Could I Have This Dance?

by Doug Haverty

A Samuel French Acting Edition

New York Hollywood London Toronto

SAMUELFRENCH.COM

Copyright © 2009 by Doug Haverty

ALL RIGHTS RESERVED

CAUTION: Professionals and amateurs are hereby warned that *COULD I HAVE THIS DANCE?* is subject to a royalty. It is fully protected under the copyright laws of the United States of America, the British Commonwealth, including Canada, and all other countries of the Copyright Union. All rights, including professional, amateur, motion picture, recitation, lecturing, public reading, radio broadcasting, television and the rights of translation into foreign languages are strictly reserved. In its present form the play is dedicated to the reading public only.

The amateur live stage performance rights to *COULD I HAVE THIS DANCE?* are controlled exclusively by Samuel French, Inc., and royalty arrangements and licenses must be secured well in advance of presentation. PLEASE NOTE that amateur royalty fees are set upon application in accordance with your producing circumstances. When applying for a royalty quotation and license please give us the number of performances intended, dates of production, your seating capacity and admission fee. Royalties are payable one week before the opening performance of the play to Samuel French, Inc., at 45 W. 25th Street, New York, NY 10010.

Royalty of the required amount must be paid whether the play is presented for charity or gain and whether or not admission is charged.

Stock royalty quoted upon application to Samuel French, Inc.

For all other rights than those stipulated above, apply to: Robert A. Freedman Dramatic Agency, 1501 Broadway, Suite 2310, New York, NY 10036.

Particular emphasis is laid on the question of amateur or professional readings, permission and terms for which must be secured in writing from Samuel French, Inc.

Copying from this book in whole or in part is strictly forbidden by law, and the right of performance is not transferable.

Whenever the play is produced the following notice must appear on all programs, printing and advertising for the play: "Produced by special arrangement with Samuel French, Inc."

Due authorship credit must be given on all programs, printing and advertising for the play.

ISBN 978-0-573-69614-5   Printed in U.S.A.   #29007

No one shall commit or authorize any act or omission by which the copyright of, or the right to copyright, this play may be impaired.

No one shall make any changes in this play for the purpose of production.

Publication of this play does not imply availability for performance. Both amateurs and professionals considering a production are strongly advised in their own interests to apply to Samuel French, Inc., for written permission before starting rehearsals, advertising, or booking a theatre.

No part of this book may be reproduced, stored in a retrieval system, or transmitted in any form, by any means, now known or yet to be invented, including mechanical, electronic, photocopying, recording, videotaping, or otherwise, without the prior written permission of the publisher.

IMPORTANT BILLING AND CREDIT REQUIREMENTS

All producers of *COULD I HAVE THIS DANCE? must* give credit to the Author of the Play in all programs distributed in connection with performances of the Play, and in all instances in which the title of the Play appears for the purposes of advertising, publicizing or otherwise exploiting the Play and/or a production. The name of the Author *must* appear on a separate line on which no other name appears, immediately following the title and *must* appear in size of type not less than fifty percent of the size of the title type.

COULD I HAVE THIS DANCE? opened on May 11, 1991 at The Colony Studio Theatre Playhouse in Los Angeles, CA. Produced by Barbara Beckley. Directed by Jules Aaron. Set design by Susan Gratch. Lighting design by Michael Gilliam. Costume design by Fontella Boone. Sound design by Tom Rincker. Assistant Director/Stage Manager: Rick Pedersen. The cast was as follows:

JEANETTE GLENDENNING	Toni Sawyer
MONICA GLENDENNING	Elizabeth Norment/Jodi Carlisle
HANK GLENDENNING	John Bluto
AMANDA GLENDENNING	Bonita Friedericy
ERROL WATKINS	Gil Johnson
COLIN MCMANN	Robert Stoeckle

COULD I HAVE THIS DANCE? opened in New York on September 9, 1993 at The Village Theatre Company, New York, New York. Directed by Jules Aaron. Set design by David Blankenship. Lighting design by Jonathan Farber. Costume design by Marj Feenan. Sound design by Jim Harrington. Stage Manager: GAK Kompes. The cast was as follows:

JEANETTE GLENDENNING	Toni Sawyer
MONICA GLENDENNING	Alyson Reim
HANK GLENDENNING	Rob Horen
AMANDA GLENDENNING	Isabel Keating
ERROL WATKINS	Randell Harris
COLIN MCMANN	Roger Michelson

CHARACTERS

(In order of appearance)

MONICA - (30s) Sharp, thorough, conservative, tough publicist and elder sister of Amanda. She is terrified of the future and romantic about what it could bring.

JEANNETTE - (60s) Beautiful, elegant, determined publicist and mother of Amanda and Monica. She can no longer see properly or speak. She is caged inside a rapidly degenerating body and cannot control her movements. (PLEASE NOTE: THIS CHARACTER DOES NOT SPEAK. SHE DANCES. See Author's Production Note.)

HANK - (60s) Mild, content, patient, retired father of Amanda and Monica and husband to Jeannette. Even though his life has been plagued with tragedy, he's managed to find the humor and love underneath.

AMANDA - (30s) Spirited, adventurous, spontaneous, brazen publicist. She keeps herself too busy to discover she's lonely. She's afraid she's not really interesting so she makes relationships brief.

ERROL - (20s) Handsome, aggressive, open, fun-loving ex-jock, currently working in the mailroom while he awaits a higher wrung on his current career ladder.

COLIN - (30s) Carefree, well-known photo-journalist. He hates phones, schedules and takes work only when he wants to. He tends to gravitate to the wrong people, but seems to like the outcome.

SETTING

The set is a fourth floor loft in Los Angeles. It is wide open with possibly large steel-and-glass windows placed high on exterior walls. There could be skylights as well.

The interior walls are white cloth; some canvas and some parachute silk. The cloth hangs on pipes suspended from ceiling and should be free flowing at the bottom so there is some movement with air currents.

The office portion of the set should include two multi-line phones, file cabinets, word processor with area dominated by large planning board and modern office utilities.

All furnishings should be sparse and white.

SCENE

The action takes place in a loft in downtown Los Angeles; the home of the Glendennings as well as the office of "Grapevine" Public Relations. The time is 1987. It is Spring.

[Please note: Although scene breaks are indicated, the actual acts should not be broken up. But rather the action should be continuous, the stage only going dark at Intermission and at final curtain].

ACT ONE
Scene 1: An Afternoon.
Scene 2: Two weeks later, evening.

ACT TWO
Scene 1: Six weeks later, late morning.
Scene 2: One month later, late morning.
Scene 3: Six weeks later, dusk.

AUTHOR'S PRODUCTION NOTE

The character of Jeannette has a degenerative nervous disease that causes her to lose control of her body movements. Normally, victims of this disease flail about waving their arms and generally have constant, jerky, spasmodic motions. It is my intention that this aspect of the disease not be depicted onstage. Rather, it should be "visible" to the characters onstage and "invisible" to the audience. The audience should see a dancer dancing the inner thoughts and emotions of Jeannette. Occasionally, her movements could become "real," but for the most part, her actions should be suggested through a rhythmic, constant waltz-like two step.

After the first scene, each scene that follows takes place at a later date. So, while it might be convenient to have the actors stay in their same costumes, it is recommended that they change costumes to help delineate the passage of time.

Jeannette's costumes should be made of some kind of fabric that displays movement well, so that when she dances in place, the image is graceful and flowing and not distracting.

The use of lighting and music in the scene changes is very important. It is recommended that the setting have ceiling fans as part of the décor. These fans twirl only during scene changes and should have lights above them that cast erratic shadows of the fan blades twirling. This effect combined with rhythmic, pulsating music should suggest a jungle feel or Latin American tropic zone where it is believed Huntington's Disease first appeared ("The Dance of Death").

ACT ONE

Scene One

(SCENE: An afternoon in Spring.)

(Lights come up to half. **MONICA** *is discovered standing at desk. She is cradling one phone and writing on the large planning board behind desk. The other phone is off the hook, lying on the desk. She is balancing a computerized mailing-list under one arm and holding a rolodex in the other. She works busily, but we do not hear her.)*

(Upstage, behind a parachute silk divider, we see the silhouette of **JEANNETTE**. *She trembles and shakes uncontrollably behind the silk.)*

(As **JEANNETTE** *moves out of silhouette into view, the lights come up in full. [Now we hear* **MONICA***].* **MONICA** *sets down the print-out and rolodex.* **JEANNETTE** *waltzes through an upstage corner noting* **MONICA***, then exits.)*

MONICA. *(into phone)* I don't care what he says, you tell him if he wants the lighting contract for Mac's next world tour, he'd better donate serious instruments and staff for this benefit...*(Phone rings)*...Right. *(She switches to another line.)* Grapevine, Monica here...That's right... Tell him: make-up call for "The Tonight Show" is 3 PM and the reporter from USA TODAY will meet him at NBC...Right...I'll be there with the schedule for Thursday. *(She picks up another phone and holds it to her other ear.)* Is he available yet?...Hello? Yes, I'm still holding...I don't care if I'm tying up his line, I refuse to play phone-tag another minute. Let it flash in his face – *(Phone rings. Into other phone)* Grapevine, Monica here...Press conference starts at two sharp. No individual interviews, no monopolizing and no flash during questions...You're the best.

(**HANK** *enters with a tall glass of water and places it next to* **MONICA**.)

HANK. Have you seen Mommy?

MONICA. *(shaking her head to* **HANK**, *then into the other receiver)* Yes, I'm still here…I'll hold!

HANK. She's loose again. *(as he starts to exit)* I can't cook, clean *and* mommy-sit.

(**HANK** *exits as* **MONICA** *speed dials a number.*)

MONICA. *(into the other receiver)* Hi, it's Monica G, the itinerary lists Mac's hotel as the Tokyo Prince, but they don't have him registered under any of his usual aliases. Did he bolt?…Thanks. *(Phone rings. Yelling offstage)* Can someone get that?

(Buzzer sounds.)

MONICA. *(into other phone)* Yes, I'm still holding, And don't you dare disconnect me. *(into other phone)* How could he check out? What about your Tokyo promoter? Don't they know where he is?

AMANDA. *(offstage, calling)* Monica? Brasilia Catering, Line 3.

(Buzzer sounds.)

MONICA. *(into phone)* Please do what you can to get that number. *(She switches lines.)* Monica here, I told you I needed a complete menu by 10 AM and it's now 11!…Fax it…I know it's a benefit, but it still has to run on schedule.

(Buzzer sounds.)

MONICA. *(calling, offstage)* Mandy, can you get the buzzer? *(Suddenly she hears what she's been waiting for on her other phone and changes tone.)* Yes? This is Monica, Hello, Bernie dear…How sweet…Well, you know I'm spearheading this benefit for "TreePeople" and – *(She waits.)* …Uh huh…We have several artists appearing and I was wondering if you'd put them up…Two nights max, I swear. *(Phone Rings)* …The Goldbergs are letting us use their Malibu Ranch…Uh huh…Of course you're invited.

AMANDA. *(offstage)* It's Mac, calling from Tokyo.

MONICA. *(covering mouthpiece, yelling offstage)* Get his number and tell him we have to have the lyrics for the theme he wrote for the benefit. *(into phone)* Bernie, everything is being donated…Of course your daughter's invited, too…No, not her roommates. Come on, Bernie, give me a break, it's a thou a head…If I need filler, I've got it.

*(**AMANDA** enters and crosses to the main entrance and exits. **MONICA** glares at her.)*

AMANDA. *(as she exits)* I'll get the buzzer.

MONICA. *(into phone)* I know how much room service he ran up last time. I'll stamp "Philanthropic" all over the menus…Thanks, I've got to jump.

*(She hangs up and phone rings. **AMANDA** enters carrying a kiwi fruit plant tucked inside the pouch of a kangaroo stuffed animal.)*

AMANDA. Turn off the bells. You gotta see this.

MONICA. *(turning off the bell, mid-ring)* What happened to Mac?

AMANDA. Oh. He moved to the promoter's house.

MONICA. Did he give you the lyrics?

AMANDA. The connection was bad.

MONICA. Mandy, I needed those lyrics first thing this morning.

AMANDA. He said, he'd have it faxed. Look. Is this cute or what? I'll bet it's from Colin. It says, "Monica: Back today, see you soon."

MONICA. Did Mac give you his number?

AMANDA. Yeah, but there was so much static, I only got half of it. What kind of plant is this?

MONICA. I'm trying to run a business and orchestrate a benefit.

AMANDA. I know, I know. You will. But look, this is so clever. It's a kiwi fruit plant. I guess that means he went to New Zealand after all.

MONICA. Yes. The major slime resurfaces again.

AMANDA. Maybe he was in the outback and couldn't get to a phone.

MONICA. Oh and what about the phones at the airport or on the plane? He'd better not show up without calling first.

AMANDA. He will because he knows that irritates you.

MONICA. That pisses me off even more.

AMANDA. I keep telling you, one night stands are the best.

MONICA. For you, yes. But –

AMANDA. Case in point: look how "happy" this six month stint has made you. Speaking of which, Nicky, I met the most tantalizing man last night. I can't get him off my mind.

MONICA. Did you say "man?"

AMANDA. Yes. He's older.

MONICA. Don't tell me you went out with someone over 21?

AMANDA. It was incredible. We skipped foreplay – well, actually the sex was the foreplay. Then he fucked my mind.

MONICA. Sounds romantic.

AMANDA. I told him about Mother and her disease. He's so refreshingly inquisitive, he just got right into my head. It was scary. He asks such simple, probing questions.

MONICA. And I hope you gave him intricate, penetrating answers? Did you tell him you're a candidate?

AMANDA. I think. You know he messed me up because I left my big bag there; the one with all the press stuff in it.

MONICA. Mandy. Now, we'll never see it again.

AMANDA. Yes, we will. He's on his way with it right now.

MONICA. What's his name?

AMANDA. Errol.

MONICA. Oh, my God. As in Flynn?

(**HANK** *re-enters with a box of envelopes.*)

HANK. Make a note. We're low on letter envelopes.

MONICA. Daddy, did you get fresh flowers for Mother?

HANK. No. Was it my turn?

MONICA. *(glaring at* **AMANDA***)* I guess not.

HANK. I'll go get some. Hey, wanna watch a video tonight?

AMANDA. Haven't you rented every movie ever made in the 60's at least three times?

HANK. Yeah, but they're so much better than anything before or after. *(to* **MONICA***)* You could pick.

MONICA. I'll watch one with you. Then I'll read to Mother.

HANK. Now we're talkin'. *(He starts to exit.)*

MONICA. Not "Easy Rider" again.

HANK. You lucked out. I loaned my copy to Vern. How about "King Rat?" *(He exits.)*

*(***ERROL*** enters carrying a large box.)*

MONICA. Hello. Are you robbing or delivering?

ERROL. If I can steal your heart, I'll deliver a sonnet.

AMANDA. This is Errol.

MONICA. The *older* man with a box of sonnets, no doubt.

AMANDA. I didn't say he –

MONICA. No, you didn't. You just referred to him as older. But you did say "man," too. *(to* **ERROL***)* Hi.

ERROL. Hi. *(to* **AMANDA***)* I'm here to set up our second date.

MONICA. What? A "second" date? This is fascinating. How'd you convince her?

ERROL. I threatened to wear my glasses, cut off my hair and pretend to be someone else.

MONICA. Well that might have fooled her once.

ERROL. Then I'd dye my hair, wear an eye-patch and limp.

MONICA. No. That would remind her too much of her fourth husband.

ERROL. *(to* **AMANDA***)* Fourth? You told me there was only three.

MONICA. She lied. Is "Errol" your real name?

ERROL. Yeah. My mom had a thing for old movie stars. My brothers are named: Spencer, Clark and Ronald.

MONICA. I can't believe you had the tenacity to show up here after surviving a date with man-eating-Mandy and

AMANDA. He's an agent. He doesn't give up.

MONICA. You are? Which agency?

ERROL. William Morris. Only I'm not an agent yet.

MONICA. Oh. Still in the mail-room, huh? How old are you?

AMANDA. *(to* **ERROL***)* You see? You see? Now you know why I don't bring anyone home. My steply ugsister gives everyone the third degree.

ERROL. I'm twenty-three.

MONICA. *(to* **AMANDA***)* Given up on seventeen year olds, have you? Going in for the more mature type, huh?

ERROL. Ten years may seem like a big difference now, but when we're 67 and 57, no one will notice.

MONICA. Look out, Mandy.

AMANDA. Don't you have to write a press release or something?

(**JEANNETTE** *dances through carrying wilted flowers. she waves them at* **MONICA** *and* **AMANDA**. *She throws them down and stops to check out* **ERROL**. *Casually,* **MONICA** *wipes the saliva off* **JEANNETTE***'s chin. Then* **JEANNETTE** *waltzes out.*)

MONICA. So, Errol, what did you major in at UCLA?

ERROL. How did you know I went to UCLA?

MONICA. That's where Mandy does all her shopping.

ERROL. Marketing.

MONICA. *(to* **AMANDA***)* Why didn't you get her fresh flowers?

AMANDA. I overslept. *(to* **ERROL***)* You kept me up too late.

ERROL. You kept me up too long. *(He laughs, then sees* **MONICA** *is not amused.)* Right. *(referring to* **JEANNETTE***)* Do you get fresh flowers for street people every day?

AMANDA. That wasn't a street person. It was my mother.

*(**ERROL** looks at **AMANDA** in amazement, then to **MONICA**.)*

MONICA. Mine, too.

ERROL. But you didn't say that she – she...

AMANDA. Don't you remember what I said last night about Huntington's Disease?

MONICA. Sometimes our retentive powers are not what they should be when all the blood is engorging other parts of our anatomy.

ERROL. No. I heard what you said, that it was a nervous disorder and I –

MONICA. Mandy, did Mac say why he's not at his hotel?

ERROL. Mac? You mean you guys do Mac, the rock star?

MONICA. Film star, poet, novelist, father, humanitarian, missing in Tokyo.

ERROL. God. He's one of my favorites. I've seen him in concert and one time, he just stopped playing and ripped off his shirt and dove into the audience. It was –

MONICA. Excuse me. I'm certain it's a fascinating recounting, but I just remembered where I might have the promoter's home number. It was neat meeting you. *(She exits.)*

ERROL. Well. I sure had your family figured all wrong.

AMANDA. How so?

ERROL. Well. Your sister is the scary one; not your mom.

AMANDA. Errol?

ERROL. Yeah?

*(**JEANNETTE** dances in again. **AMANDA** looks away. **ERROL** watches her, fascinated. **JEANNETTE** carries a child's plastic cup with cover and straw. She tries to hand it to **AMANDA** who reaches for it, but they don't connect. The cup falls. **ERROL** reaches down and picks it up. He tries to hand it to **JEANNETTE**.)*

AMANDA. She needs a refill. Mom, this is Errol. We met last night.

ERROL. Hey there, Mrs. Glendenning. *(He puts a hand out to shake.* **JEANNETTE** *just waltzes in place, looking suspicious.)*

AMANDA. She doesn't...she can't.

ERROL. How come she's shaking all over like that?

AMANDA. This is why I don't do second dates.

ERROL. *(yelling to* **JEANNETTE***)* Mrs. G, it's nice to meet you.

AMANDA. She can hear you fine.

ERROL. Can she see me?

AMANDA. Yes. She just has occasional trouble focusing.

ERROL. Anyone would if they lurched around like they were being electrocuted.

(to **JEANNETTE***)* Don't you get tired?

*(***JEANNETTE** *appears to laugh, then looks at* **AMANDA.***)*

AMANDA. She can't stop.

ERROL. Even, like, at night when she sleeps? *(***AMANDA** *shakes her head. Then to* **JEANNETTE***)* God. I'm so sorry.

*(***JEANNETTE** *smiles at* **AMANDA.***)*

ERROL. This is a put on, right? Anybody tries to stretch the second date rule gets this jack-hammer dance?

*(***ERROL** *tries to hold* **JEANNETTE** *still. She continues waltzing, but he reacts as if he was touching a strong, trembling man in shock.)*

God.

*(***JEANNETTE** *smiles and exits.)*

ERROL. How many people have this?

AMANDA. About a hundred thousand in the U.S. More overseas.

ERROL. No shit?

AMANDA. In Venezuela, where they think it started, whole villages have it because they're so inbred.

ERROL. Unreal.

AMANDA. They also call it, "The Dance of Death." Woodie Guthrie had it. Arlo is at risk.

ERROL. Do you have it?

AMANDA. Does it look like I have it? What do you think? Take my temperature, maybe it's coming on. Did my eye just twitch or it starting? Did I drop that pencil or am I losing control? Did I forget to pick up the dry cleaning or is it the disease? *(beat)* Does it look like I have it?

ERROL. No, but come to think of it, you did some trembling last night that was awfully flattering.

AMANDA. It isn't always passed on. There's a 50/50 chance that I have the gene.

ERROL. So, you just have to sit and wait for...

AMANDA. Signs, symptoms. But I don't sit or wait.

ERROL. God. There is something majorly wrong with me.

AMANDA. What?

ERROL. I'm getting turned on here.

AMANDA. Errol! Leave.

ERROL. Does it hurt?

AMANDA. This is not going to work.

ERROL. How come there's all that pain in her face?

AMANDA. Frustration. *(beat)* There's still an intelligent person in there; a lady who started a P.R. firm twenty years ago with one client and ran it out of a converted service porch. Now we have twenty clients with a waiting list and she can't run it. And she can't hold still. And that frustrates her more than anything.

ERROL. You mean it could kick in any minute?

AMANDA. Yes. Usually it starts with middle age, whenever that is.

(**ERROL** *kisses* **AMANDA.** *They kiss briefly, then she breaks it.*)

AMANDA. Errol, I'm sorry I told you. It's not having the desired effect.

ERROL. You thought I'd freak and fly, huh?

AMANDA. Last night was an unforgettable time for me. I'd like to keep it that way. Let's just –

ERROL. You're not going to get rid of me that easily. I like you.

AMANDA. You only think you like me because I said that I'd only go out once. That's a dangerous thing for me to do. Because it stimulates some kind of challenge mechanism –

ERROL. Okay. You're right. I'll have to admit your ultimatum was sort of competitively intriguing. And I guess I'm just average in the end, right?

AMANDA. Not in the end or the middle or the top. No.

ERROL. Better than?

AMANDA. Much.

ERROL. So how much better than would a guy have to be to break the one date rule?

AMANDA. It's not a question of…I just want to have unencumbered fun…while I can. Okay, Errol?

ERROL. Call me "Err." *[Pronounced 'air'].*

AMANDA. Err? Okay. Great. Err, babe. I've got to get back to work. Thanks for –

ERROL. Amanda, I'll tell you something. I've always liked older girls.

AMANDA. Oh, God. You would have to go and call me a 'girl.'

ERROL. See, I'm the oldest and my brothers and my parents always expected me to know what to do and how to act. But I like being younger sometimes and having that burden lifted.

AMANDA. So, what are you sticking around for? Do you want to see if I get to waltz the Dance of Death? Let's have three or four kids and make them wonder if they'll get it or escape? Yes! Let's go out. I'm game. Sure. I'll break my rule.

ERROL. Sorry that I don't have any big phobia about this. It's not that I don't appreciate the significance of it, I –

AMANDA. Come on, Err. Who are you kidding? *(She moves to phone and turns on bells.)*

ERROL. Yeah. You're right. We'd probably get divorced in ten years anyway; fifteen tops. So – *(He stops when he realizes his joke has hurt her.)* I'm not asking to marry you, just to hang out.

AMANDA. I know...no. *(The phone rings.* **AMANDA** *exits running.)*

ERROL. *(calling after her)* What do I say when I answer?

AMANDA. *(offstage)* "Grapevine."

ERROL. *(into phone)* Grrrapevine...I don't know...*The* Chevy Chase?...No, really?...Yeah, well...Okay...She has your number?...Okay...Good...I'll tell her...No. I won't forget, ever...Bye. *(***ERROL*** starts writing a message.)*

HANK. *(offstage)* In through here.

COLIN. *(offstage)* Thanks.

*(***HANK*** enters still in his jogging clothes, carrying videos and flowers.* **COLIN** *enters behind him carrying a shopping bag filled with library books and papers.* **ERROL** *hangs up.)*

HANK. Yeah, she's – Oh, well. She was here. Son, have you seen Monica?

ERROL. Yes.

HANK. *(noticing* **ERROL***'s message pad)* Is that message pad used up already? Crimenutley! These carbonless things are the most expensive waste-basket filler-uppers man ever created. Now me? I prefer a spindle. *(to* **COLIN***)* Just wait here. *(He exits.)*

COLIN. Uh, Hi. I'm Colin McMann.

ERROL. Errol Watkins.

COLIN. Could you buzz Monica and tell her I'm here?

ERROL. No.

COLIN. She's not here?

ERROL. I can't buzz her.

COLIN. Why?

ERROL. I don't know how.

COLIN. *(yelling)* Monica!

MONICA. *(offstage)* That better not be Colin.

COLIN. *(yelling)* No. It's – uh – Errol. I'm practicing yelling like Colin. *(to* **ERROL***)* How long have you been with Mandy and Monica?

ERROL. What time is it?

COLIN. Four?

ERROL. Thirty-six hours.

COLIN. Oh. What do they have you do besides refuse to buzz them?

ERROL. I don't work *for* them.

COLIN. Oh. I see.

ERROL. What do you do besides refuse to use the intercom?

COLIN. I'm a photographer.

ERROL. And you take pictures for them?

COLIN. Of them. They're real kinky and I'm the only one they let in to...You know...snap them. Are you posing with them today?

*(***ERROL*** gets very uneasy.* **MONICA** *enters.)*

ERROL. No. I...really? You're –

MONICA. *(turning her back to* **COLIN***)* Errol Flynn, don't believe a word this ungentleman says.

ERROL. You mean he lies on top of every other rude thing he does?

MONICA. Yes. *(to* **ERROL***)* What did you do with Mandy?

ERROL. You mean last night? That's kind of personal.

MONICA. No. I meant now.

ERROL. She ran away.

MONICA. I told you she was afraid of second dates.

ERROL. No. I asked her out for #3, 4, 5 and 6. I made a schedule – I know, spontaneity gets shot to shit, but – it's all planned out: places, menus, movies, music, beds, oils. She went into severe filofax-shock.

MONICA. I'll bet she did.

ERROL. It's only because I totally accept her Huntington's stuff. She never banked on that. She can't handle it so it zoo's her out when someone else can.

MONICA. *(to* **COLIN***)* You know dropping by unannounced is sneered upon.

COLIN. Which made dropping by somewhat announced all the more enticing. Did you get my Kanga-gram?

MONICA. Why didn't you just return my calls like I requested?

COLIN. You know how they say that when you sneeze it takes a minute off the end of your life? Well, every time I call here, I spend an eternity on hold. And each second I spend on hold takes an *hour* off the end of my life. I'm not young enough to chance many calls to you.

MONICA. You blew an hour coming downtown. Then the drive back to the beach will be –

COLIN. Yeah. But hold time is passive. Going downtown is an event; it's active. You really begin to see L.A. after you've spent two weeks in New Zealand.

MONICA. Since you're here, I'll tell you what we need. Then you're free to evaporate again.

COLIN. *(to* **ERROL***)* Be careful. That nasty barb is ricocheting all over the room.

*(***ERROL** *ducks.)*

MONICA. Errol? I want you to sit down at that desk. Press the first speed dial button and say, "Grapevine, checking in." They will then give you a long list of names and phone numbers.

ERROL. No kidding. You'd let me do that?

MONICA. You can even put it on your resume.

ERROL. I could, couldn't I? *(He moves to desk and gets situated.)*

COLIN. *(to* **MONICA***)* Looks like you're busy.

MONICA. Average.

COLIN. Anything doing tonight?

ERROL. *(watching* **COLIN** *and* **MONICA** *until* **MONICA** *glances at him, then into phone)* "Grapevine, checking out – I mean, in…Okay. *(He writes volumes during the next scene.)*

MONICA. You know damn well my life is planned months in advance and you expect to waltz in here and arrange a date the same day?

COLIN. I don't have to be anywhere. My calendar for this evening is deliberately clear.

MONICA. What makes you think I don't have plans?

COLIN. Because I know what your forehead looks like if you do. There's a network of furrowed brows that send very specific signals. And right now I'm receiving hostility, embarrassment, bewilderment, hunger, anger, lust, more anger, matching empty calendar...rage.

MONICA. I don't feel like eating.

COLIN. We won't eat.

MONICA. I don't feel like chatting.

COLIN. We'll draw pictures. *(He tries to kiss her.)* Hey. I'm sorry. I told you when we met that I was an inconsiderate asshole.

MONICA. And you've proved it.

COLIN. But despite everything I've done – or haven't done – I care.

MONICA. You do?

COLIN. I know I have a weird way of showing it. In the past six months, I –

MONICA. A simple phone call – or a fax if you're so spineless you can't voice a feeble excuse. I wish you hadn't come. *(She starts to exit.)*

COLIN. Wait.

MONICA. What?

COLIN. You're making me mad.

MONICA. Good. Then you won't mind storming out.

COLIN. Something else is bothering you.

MONICA. What does it matter? I'm not some special camera lens you occasionally screw on.

COLIN. Hm. What's the operative word here? Occasionally? Camera?

MONICA. What am I? Someone you fill an empty calendar with?

COLIN. How can you say that to someone who asked you to move in with them?

MONICA. You asked a month ago. I haven't heard from you in two weeks. What am I supposed to think?

COLIN. I told you I was going on assignment in New Zealand.

MONICA. You said you might. You said you'd let me know. You said you'd call.

(JEANNETTE *dances in quickly to* MONICA *shaking her head.*)

MONICA. What's the matter?

(JEANNETTE *shakes her head and points to her stomach.*)

MONICA. What is it? Are you sick?

(JEANNETTE *shakes her head and points to her mouth.*)

MONICA. I don't know, Mom. Settle down.

HANK. *(offstage)* Nettie?

(JEANNETTE *dances off.*)

COLIN. I thought a lot about you when I was in Tasmania, too.

MONICA. Did you think about picking up a phone?

HANK. *(offstage, calling)* Nettie?

COLIN. I couldn't, see? It's this vicious cycle of remorse. I like being your sexual slave, but I can't take the phone abuse.

MONICA. What the hell are you talking about?

COLIN. Okay. Hypothetical Call #1: "Hi, Nicky? I'm leaving for New Zealand tomorrow." "What? How come you didn't tell me? I've made all these plans and now – Shit!" Then, deafening silence. So, I avoid phone call #1. Then, feeling terribly guilty, I consider Phone Call #2: "Hi, Nicky. It's Colin. I'm calling from New Zealand." "What?! How come you didn't tell me? I've made plans and now – Shit!!" Then, deafening, international, expensive silence. Then, every day I kick myself for not jumping into the icy cold phone waters the day before. And every day it gets harder.

HANK. *(offstage, calling)* Nettie?

COLIN. So, I tried not to dwell on it, do my work and hope I could come here and somehow make up for my complete disregard for your feelings and throw myself at your feet.

MONICA. Stomping on you is tempting, but it won't make up for –

HANK. *(as he enters carrying large plastic covered glass with thick straw)* Did Mommy just fly through here?

MONICA. Yes. She seemed upset.

HANK. She hates this pureed spinach, but she can't survive on fruit smoothies. She's got to have her greens. *(to* **COLIN***)* Say, Colin. Did I mention we loved the Kanga.

COLIN. Glad someone did.

MONICA. Maybe you didn't put enough vinegar in. She likes vinegar on her spinach.

HANK. Right. I'll doctor it up. Then I have to catch her. I made too much, you want some? *(offering glass to* **COLIN.***)*

COLIN. Uh, no thanks. I had mashed broccoli on the plane.

HANK. Your loss. *(as he exits, calling)* Nettie?

MONICA. So, now. Where were we?

COLIN. You had just flown into Tirade #12, you know, the one about my disappearing into –

MONICA. Had I finished?

COLIN. No. Tirade twelve goes on much longer. There's the part about how obviously mismatched we are, how inconsiderate I am…how patient you are. How we both deserve better –

MONICA. Oh, yeah. And that's where you usually walk out. Well before you slam the door off its hinges, the reason I called is that Mac really liked your session. We need new pictures for "Interview" magazine and he requested you. Do you "feel" like it?

COLIN. There you go, jumping from –

MONICA. So will you shoot Mac?

COLIN. When?

MONICA. You say. We'll work something out.

COLIN. I don't know. I can't think. Yeah, I guess. But, Monica –

MONICA. And I'd like you to cover my benefit for "Tree-People."

COLIN. But that's not for three months, isn't it? I can't book that far ahead.

MONICA. I'll remind you as the date gets closer.

ERROL. *(hangs up)* Shit. You got some serious heavyweights calling you, lady.

MONICA. Yes, but the ones I want to call, never do.

ERROL. Mac called from Tokyo, something about a benefit. You know I do a great Mac impersonation, "Fall on me, just close your eyes and baby…"

COLIN. Was there a message from me there?

ERROL. What's your name, again?

COLIN. Colin.

ERROL. Right. *(checking)* Yeah.

COLIN. So, you see? I did call.

MONICA. And it probably took a year off your life, huh? So, you phoned. Had to make sure we were here before you trucked downtown.

COLIN. I called you from the UCLA Medical Library.

ERROL. My ol' haunting grounds! UCLA, I mean, not the Med –

MONICA. Library, we know.

COLIN. I met this guy in Auckland and he told me one his of neighbors had Huntington's and that there were all kinds of developments and new tests and –

MONICA. And so you had to verify everything I told you; make sure I was accurate; you needed to know every detail before you could properly consider…make certain it's not contagious, couldn't be sexually transmitted –

COLIN. Monica.

ERROL. It's not, is it?

MONICA. Only if you climax at the same time.

(ERROL *thinks a beat, then looks puzzled.*)

Can't recall, huh Tiger?

ERROL. Well, there –

MONICA. Too many simo-climaxes, I know.

COLIN. I realize you're being snide because you're scared of any new developments. So, I now accept the apology you'll give me.

MONICA. Wait a minute, wait a minute. Now, I'm having a little difficulty here picturing this nomadic photographer at a library. I thought you hated taking notes and writing reports and that's why you gave up journalism.

COLIN. Half right. I always loved the research part. I just hated the compiling part.

MONICA. So you got off the plane and played sleuth, huh?

COLIN. No. I did research in New Zealand and then more this morning. Is that what you wanted to hear?

MONICA. It is. I assume you've had some degree of success since you've risked being pummeled at my feet.

COLIN. It's news. In the past two months, they've made some headway in testing.

MONICA. That's encouraging.

ERROL. *(to MONICA)* Hey. Don't you think you should get Amanda?

MONICA. Maybe by the time I'm 91, they'll have a vaccine.

COLIN. That, I don't know about.

ERROL. She'd want to know.

MONICA. No she wouldn't.

ERROL. Yes she would.

MONICA. Oh. You humped her one night and all of a sudden you an expert?

ERROL. Even if we hadn't, I'd know…Just from talking to – Go on. I just want you to make sure she's okay. I said something kinda mean and…

MONICA. *(glaring at* **COLIN***)* We have tour press packets to mail out today and we need to update the address file before we print out the mailing labels and – *(She stops.)* Testing…*(She exits.* **COLIN** *starts to go after her, but decides not to.)*

ERROL. Man. She must be something else in the sack, huh?

COLIN. Why do you say that?

ERROL. Well, I mean for you to put up with that shit.

COLIN. Oh. I enjoy Nick. She's like a feisty wine.

ERROL. Oh. Well, I don't get it. 'Course I'm not into wine.

COLIN. You don't think she's sexy?

ERROL. Well, yeah. They both are, but 'ol Nicker's personality is a real turn off. She's like a barracuda.

COLIN. Yeah, maybe that's what I like about her.

ERROL. My Grandpa used to go deep sea fishing and he said that struggling with a barracuda was like keeping it up for two hours – a real endurance test. And he said there's a point when the fish gives it everything its got and you ride that test of strength till your arms, back and butt ache. Then you're one.

COLIN. I've never –

ERROL. So, once you've swallowed that nasty, bitter wine, don't you want to knock back something smoother?

COLIN. No. I'm perverse. You begin to crave the edginess. And it gets smoother.

ERROL. Oh, so you're into this, kinda, "verbal" S & M?

COLIN. You know, a lot of people in our business think Monica's very sexy. And no one could get to her. And, at first it was this competitive thing. Like, I'll do it, I'll get there. And I did. And then, just to prove it wasn't a heartless quest, I stayed. It amazed everyone, but a funny thing happened. I got to see a side of her she doesn't show anyone. And I got hooked.

*(***HANK*** enters, still in jogging clothes, carrying office supplies. He sets them down.)*

COLIN. Hi, Hank.

HANK. 'Lo, boys.

ERROL. Hi. I'm Errol.

HANK. I'm sure.

ERROL. How's it goin'?

HANK. I've had better decades.

ERROL. How long you been retired now, Mr. G?

HANK. Retired? I work seven days a week, 52 weeks a year.

ERROL. Oh. You mean helping with the business.

HANK. That and watching Jeannette. It's a full-time job.

COLIN. What would you be doing if you weren't committed – so to speak?

HANK. Camp. Bird-watch. I took Nettie with me one time, sort of a trial. Whew. What a mistake. She did not like it. She thrashed that tent within an inch of its life. Somebody thought a bear got to it. She scared the birds, too.

ERROL. I'll bet. Oh.

HANK. I'd just like to drive. Just get in the car with all my gear. No plans, no phone numbers, no check-in points. Just go. *(beat)* I'll get to it.

ERROL. Amanda told me you love looking after your Mrs. G; that you refused a nurse.

HANK. True. I didn't want a nurse, that was because of her. But "love" looking after Nettie? Nah.

ERROL. Is it hard?

HANK. Of course it is. What kind of question is that? If you're trying to make conversation, don't bother. It's not necessary. If you want to talk to me, ask something spicy.

ERROL. Okay. Do you still have sex with your wife?

HANK. *(smiles)* What do you think?

ERROL. I don't know. I know old people do it.

HANK. We do, huh? You knew that?

ERROL. Yeah. My grandfather told me.

HANK. I see. Well…it's tricky.

ERROL. I'll bet. Oh. You mean tricky to talk about or do?

HANK. Both.

COLIN. Hank, you don't have to –

HANK. Ya see, the hard part is holding her still.

COLIN. I can imagine.

HANK. You got to hold her, see, and get into her rhythm.

ERROL. But does she like it? I mean, can you tell?

HANK. *(to* **COLIN***)* He's obviously very inexperienced. *(to* **ERROL***)* Son, I always know when a lady likes my lovemaking. You develop a sense for this. Yes. She likes it. You know the disease makes her arms and legs go like crazy and she can't talk or read or watch TV, but she's still a person inside with needs and desires and love. And let me tell you, once you get in rhythm with that buckin' bronco, it's like being swallowed by an epileptic hooker.

(beat)

I don't mean any disrespect by that. It's just the only way I can describe it and I'm not used to describing it. But you asked.

ERROL. Right.

(beat)

COLIN. I go on trips like you talked about all the time. I never thought of them as someone's dream. They're just assignments. Get pictures, fill pages. If you'd like to come with me sometime –

HANK. Nah. The beauty is to be able to go alone. Maybe I'll fill in for you. *(He exits.)*

ERROL. Have you…touched her?

COLIN. Who?

ERROL. The mother, Mrs. G – Nettie.

COLIN. Not really. She –

ERROL. I did. It was – Well, my Grandma has this little dog and it likes to dry hump your leg, you know? But if you put your hand on that little dog's back during the hump, it's all full of tension almost like a current was charging through it.

COLIN. What were you doing?

ERROL. I was just trying to stop her from shaking.

COLIN. Did you?

ERROL. No. *(beat)* Does that freak you out, to see the Mom like that and know they could get...you know?

*(**AMANDA** and **MONICA** re-enter.)*

AMANDA. What? What? Tell me.

MONICA. Make it fast.

COLIN. They've come up with a test they can give you now to determine if you'll develop Huntington's.

AMANDA. What?

MONICA. Do they pinpoint the day so you can plan the good part of your life?

COLIN. No. They can't –

AMANDA. Is it 100% conclusive?

COLIN. 99%

MONICA. A test. Great. Maybe they'll find a cure one of these centuries.

AMANDA. This is really scary. You know, for so long, I just put it out of my mind – the possibility. *(to **ERROL**)* I just pretend like it's not a factor in my life. But to know, once and for all...When can we go?

COLIN. You mean you'd want to take the test?

AMANDA. Yes! Now. Within the hour! Do I have to fly to Switzerland or – ?

COLIN. They can do it right here. All they need is a sample of your blood and your parents.

MONICA. Mandy, wait. Are you sure you want to know?

AMANDA. Are you kidding? Absofuckinglutely yes!

MONICA. No.

AMANDA. No what?

MONICA. I don't want to know.

AMANDA. But Nicky, you could really plan. At last someone will say, "Monica, in fifteen years your life is turning to shit. So, live it up! Charge it! Buy now, pay never!" Or they might say, "Miss Glendenning, I'm sorry. You're not in the will. This legacy has not been passed on to you." At which time the entire UCLA Boys Choir comes in with their best "Hallelujahs" and there'd be a parade with those people who twirl and eat fire and confetti –

MONICA. Mandy, settle down. Think for a second. What if that test's not hallelujah-worthy?

AMANDA. Then it won't be any worse than it is now.

MONICA. Yes it will. At least now we have hope.

AMANDA. Monica. I've spent thirty-four years putting off a life because I didn't know if I'd have one. I don't want to spend another minute in the dark. Colin, where do – ?

COLIN. Here, I've Xeroxed some articles. *(He reaches into his bag and pulls out a folder.* **MONICA** *snatches it from him.)*

MONICA. What are the chances, huh? Little sister doesn't have it. Probably big sister got all the crummy genes. *(beat)* If you take away my hope, I'll have nothing.

AMANDA. Monica. Give me the folder.

MONICA. No.

AMANDA. We'll discuss this calmly.

MONICA. *(to* **COLIN***)* How could you do this? Now, see what I'll have to live with? Now it's not only, "Will I get it? Won't I? How bad? How soon?" but it's, "Should I take the test or shouldn't I?"

COLIN. I thought I was bringing you good news.

AMANDA. It is! It's a chance at good news.

ERROL. You know, I had to take a blood test when I joined William Morris. The clinic had a poster of sky and the trick is to look away from bloodsucker. Don't watch. Just stare at the poster...or whatever.

(They all stare at **ERROL** *in amazement.)*

I did catch a glimpse out of the corner of my eye. I saw this little jet of blood squirt into the tube. See, now that made me queasy.

MONICA. It's not taking the blood that – *(She stops. Then, to* **AMANDA***)* He must be incredibly sensitive in bed.

COLIN. I don't care if you take it. I only wanted to let you know the opportunity exists.

MONICA. I don't mean to sound ungrateful, but I never wanted to know.

AMANDA. Why?

MONICA. Because I...I'm sorry, Colin. Thanks for the offer. Thanks for the research. You went to a lot of trouble. I'm behaving like an idiot.

AMANDA. I'll say.

MONICA. I said it. You don't have to underline it.

(beat)

COLIN. Errol, come on. I think the sisters here need some time to themselves.

AMANDA. No. I want to –

MONICA. Yes. We'd like that.

AMANDA. *(to COLIN and MONICA)* Why are you trying to get rid of everyone? Do you think you can talk me out of this? My mind's made up and there's no need to –

MONICA. Yes there is, godammit! I need to talk this over. Is that too much to ask? Can you get laid later and give me a little time here?

(AMANDA starts to exit. COLIN stops her.)

COLIN. Amanda, please. I didn't mean to start a sister war.

AMANDA. There will be no war. No debate even. I have to know. It's possible to know and I will. It's just a matter of how soon. If Big Sis want to keep the mystery, that's her business. I think she actually likes the not-knowing. It gives her something to grouse about.

MONICA. Mandy, shut up.

ERROL. You think it's safe to leave these two alone?

COLIN. No, but it's more dangerous to stay.

ERROL. *(as he hands AMANDA a photograph)* Here's a Polaroid from last night. You can use it to distract you during the test. My number's on the bottom.

MONICA. *(to ERROL)* She's got your number. Bye, boys.

(ERROL exits.)

COLIN. I'll drop by about...seven?

MONICA. Colin, I told you –

COLIN. I know. If you're busy, I'll watch "Easy Rider" with Hank. *(He exits.)*

AMANDA. How long have you known about this test?

MONICA. Just now. When Colin –

AMANDA. No bullshit, Nick. I know you too well.

MONICA. It's not like I chained you to a bedpost. You're at UCLA every night. You could have slipped into the library just as easily. I didn't withhold information from you.

AMANDA. You knew. You chose to stay in the dark, but you had 2,000 opportunities to casually discuss it with me.

MONICA. I read somewhere in the countless articles I've scoured that testing was taking place, but Mandy, that's all they do is test, test, test. *(beat)* It's only recently become available. I figured you wouldn't ever want to know. You play Russian roulette with sex, why know if there's a bullet in the chamber of your forty-sixth year?

(beat)

AMANDA. You're right. I shouldn't have depended on you to be my medical advisor. You've only been that since I was three. Stupid, stupid me. *(beat)*

MONICA. All right. I did know about the testing process, but it's very complicated. It's not like going in and having them stab your finger and determining your blood type.

AMANDA. I didn't think it would be.

MONICA. There's counseling and neurological, psychological exams –

AMANDA. You mean I can't just run in and ask for my fate and get my parking validated?

MONICA. There's a catch. They need the blood of a sibling, too.

AMANDA. Why can't they just examine my blood and Mom's and see – ?

MONICA. They need two generations of blood samples to compare yours to.

AMANDA. Fine. Then we'll all go in. It'll be a family letting.

MONICA. I can't believe we're actually…When I first read about this, I thought, "My God. How will I ever convince Mandy to take this test so *I*'ll know?" I was so certain you'd never want to glimpse at…

AMANDA. So you *do* want to know?

MONICA. No.

AMANDA. Okay. Well, do they have to tell you? Say they sampled all our blood and gave me my results. Couldn't they keep yours a secret?

MONICA. *(beat)* They could.

AMANDA. Monica, three months ago, what did you tell me you wanted more than anything in the world?

MONICA. I don't know. My wish list changes daily.

AMANDA. No. You have catalogues of baby clothes, furniture, toys. You have a book of the Best Baby Names. You subscribe to "Parents" magazine –

MONICA. It's a professional subscription.

AMANDA. Who are you kidding? You could take that test and if you're clear, put that anxious baby-maker to work.

MONICA. If I decide to have a baby, it won't be because I've taken this goddam test.

AMANDA. You can't be serious. You couldn't possibly consider passing this seed along.

MONICA. Why not? Are we so terrible? Is it such a bad deal to offer someone forty-six good years?

AMANDA. Yes! It's half a life!

MONICA. Not necessarily. Some people live to be ninety or a hundred and they never live a full life.

AMANDA. It would be the ultimate act of selfishness.

MONICA. And abortion isn't?

AMANDA. *(beat)* Is there a problem here? Monica, are you – ?

MONICA. No. Good God. I just came close and…I keep coming close.

(**JEANNETTE** *waltzes in and offers white rose to* **MONICA.**)

AMANDA. Well, then. All the more reason to finally know. *(She takes folders and exits.)*

(JEANNETTE dances around MONICA.)

MONICA. Oh, right. Ply me with flowers. I remember when you were stingy with your precious roses. We weren't supposed to play near them. And you always spied on us. I pretended that we were living on another planet and that I was your prisoner. All the lives of people on Earth depended on those flowers. Each new bud meant we could live another day. You were the evil space queen in the "Venution Ruling Structure." But I knew you'd release me.

(JEANNETTE takes the flower and smells it as she dances. Her dancing slows slightly. MONICA tries to hold on to JEANNETTE.)

MONICA. Twenty years ago, if someone told you you could have a blood test to see if this disease would hit you, would you have wanted to know?

(JEANNETTE considers this with astonishment, then shakes her head violently and breaks away from MONICA.)

MONICA. Neither would I. But that test exists. I could know.

(JEANNETTE shakes her head violently as she dances. Then she stops and looks at MONICA forlornly. Then she hits herself several times.)

MONICA. Mother, don't. Don't.

(JEANNETTE rips the rose apart and waltzes out. MONICA looks at the scattered rose petals. She bends down and picks up a few, then stops and reflects. JEANNETTE re-enters unseen and watches MONICA.)

(Lights fade to half. MONICA exits. [Any necessary scene or properties adjustment may take place now, behind JEANNETTE.] In the half-light, JEANNETTE begins to shake and tremble violently. She reaches out for the exiting MONICA. She crosses to the window and looks outside, longingly. She is trapped and angry. She exits.)

(Lights up from half to full.)
(It is now:)

Scene Two

(SCENE: Two weeks later, evening.)

(A breeze billows the curtains in the loft. **COLIN** *and* **MONICA** *are seated at a low table, finishing dinner and looking at a scrapbook* **COLIN** *has brought over. Candles are lit and they seem relaxed.)*

MONICA. God. Your parents *were* older.

COLIN. Yeah. I was kind of an afterthought-ish accident, I think. They were trying to retire and travel so I took a lot of pictures while they were home.

MONICA. They never took you with them?

COLIN. No. They'd stick me with one of my older sisters. I look at these pictures and try to know them, but I don't.

MONICA. So, to spite your parents you'll be the best father knows best.

COLIN. Yeah. *(He laughs.)* And my mother carried this little grandchild family tree hot-pad. It has raised tree branches with her kids' names and then little clear picture holes for grand-fruit-children.

MONICA. She sounds adorable.

COLIN. She was so proud of it. She filled all the fruit-shaped holes with pictures of her grandkids and showed that tree to every stranger she met. *(beat)* But…she didn't know those kids. In their travels, they didn't stop and see them, only paraded their photos.

MONICA. Oh, God. My dolls were Mother's grandchildren. She'd see me pushing them in a buggy and say, "How many grandkids do you have for me today?" No matter how many I had in there, it was never enough. And now I…

COLIN. What?

MONICA. Nothing. Sometimes I think about her back then. I…She seems like a different person. She was the "Mom" then – very much in charge – and now I…

COLIN. But she's such a big part of your life, that's great. Even when my parents were alive, we were so loose knit, I knew neighbors better.

MONICA. So, that's why you keep coming back. It's not for me, it's for the tight knit family.

COLIN. You got me. *(beat)* But Nick. What's really bothering you?

MONICA. Well. We're – *(She stops.)* I'm just nervous about the press conference tonight. Sure you don't want to go with?

COLIN. Yes. I'm sure. Do *you* have to – ?

MONICA. I promised. It's her first play since she won the Academy Award and she's terrified everyone will be out to crucify her.

COLIN. So what will you do, burn the crosses?

MONICA. And I thought you might like to meet my god-daughter.

COLIN. Aha. That's the real reason. God-mother pays a visit.

MONICA. Sally and her mom have promised to help out with the "TreePeople" benefit and –

COLIN. You're really going all out for this benefit, aren't you?

MONICA. Not really.

COLIN. Donating all your services?

MONICA. Well, yes.

COLIN. Don't you usually just reduce your fee?

MONICA. Sometimes, I…

COLIN. What's so special about this one?

MONICA. I don't know. I guess I just wanted to – I felt the need to accept some responsibility.

COLIN. You're the Responsibility Queen. You run this place and your family and –

MONICA. Okay, but it's mine. I thought I should do something for someone else. I stacked up my accomplishments one time when you were MIA and they were all "me" things. And so I asked myself, "You're thirty-six, what have you done?" Once I decided to do something useful, I shopped around for the lucky benefactor. I thought about the Brazilian Rain Forest or whales or Indians and I settled on "TreePeople." I mass produce vast quantities of printed paper, so I thought I should replenish. Planting new trees seemed clean, helpful. Air might be a milliliter cleaner for children. *(beat)* So, will you come with me tonight? I've told everyone about you and they think I've concocted you like some press release.

COLIN. Will you be happy if *we* go to this soiree?

MONICA. If *we* go, yes.

COLIN. How happy?

(She kisses him. She breaks the kiss.)

What?

MONICA. I'm suspicious.

COLIN. Of?

MONICA. Things going too well. You.

COLIN. Understandable.

MONICA. You're here now, you'll go with me tonight. You've asked me to move in with you, but in – ?

COLIN. So many doubts. Stop worrying about next year. Just –

MONICA. I can't help it. I'm planning, "If he moves in, which drawers could I empty?" "Should I convert half the closet to double racks?" "Should we get our own place?" "Should I move to the beach?"

COLIN. I'm flattered I'm even in your plans.

MONICA. Yeah. You are. Last week I was planning on how to kill you.

*(**COLIN** touches her hair, then her face.)*

COLIN. So severe, always full of extremes.

MONICA. Why are you here?

COLIN. I've been asking that for six months.

MONICA. You're a hotshot photographer who could have anyone. You probably have a file with phone numbers right out of Cosmo.

COLIN. I called them and they're all busy tonight.

MONICA. Asshole.

(COLIN kisses MONICA. They break.)

MONICA. So, how many women have you actually moved in together with?

COLIN. You mean in my life or this month?

MONICA. Both.

COLIN. Let's see. I'd have to think.

MONICA. Need more than ten fingers?

COLIN. Three.

MONICA. Ever come close to the 'm' thing?

COLIN. Once.

MONICA. Cold feet?

COLIN. No…yeah. See, sibling pressure runs intense in my family and everyone was propagating. I'd been dating this one lady for about six months and I decided to propose. It was New Year's Eve and she was cooking an elegant dinner for two. I'd made a deposit on a ring and went to pick it up. But I couldn't go into the shop. I went around the block seven times. Eventually, they closed.

MONICA. You didn't *not* show up for dinner?

COLIN. Oh, we had a great dinner and I gave her this portable CD player she wanted. I guess, subconsciously, we both thought it was going to be a significant evening. She picked up on that. I didn't want to disappoint her.

MONICA. You mean she thought you were going to propose?

COLIN. Yes.

MONICA. Well, *I've* certainly cooked that dinner. I never got a CD player though. Should I put in my order now?

COLIN. You didn't cook tonight.

MONICA. So that's why the handsome, single, photographer never lets his hopeful dinner dates cook for him. He's run out of CD players.

(He kisses her. She stops him.)

Is it the French wine or the French-kissing that intoxicates me?

COLIN. My tongue is marinated. I practically drank all the wine myself. *(They kiss. He starts to undo her blouse.)*

MONICA. Yes. We should change. What will you wear?

COLIN. Wait. You're doing it. Stop planning.

MONICA. I'm not.

COLIN. Yes, you are. *(He walks away.)* Just once I'd like to kiss you and not hear the gears churning.

MONICA. What?

COLIN. Really. I feel you, I know what's going on up there. Your brain is saying: "Hmm. Pleasant sensation on the lips. Oh. Here comes the tongue. Did I floss? That reminds me, I've got to schedule that dental cleaning and the insurance premiums are due. Ooh. He's fondling my breast. Where's Mother? Oh, it's okay. Hm. That feels nice. I've got to rinse the rest of the dishes, do something with my hair, and I still haven't gotten a confirmation from Barbara Walters! Maybe I should do something for him. Where's his zipper? No. There's not enough time."

MONICA. Colin, stop.

COLIN. It's true, isn't it? You can't turn it off. That planning program in your computer brain operates twenty-four hours a day.

MONICA. It's not like –

COLIN. *(angrily)* Is it too much to ask to have your full attention?

MONICA. You do. It's just split. See, when I'm on the phone or something and I'm talking about promo schedules or press days, those wheels are turning and I'm thinking about you.

COLIN. Sure. Wondering why I'm late or where I am or how can you convince me into going to an opening with you.

MONICA. I'll try.

COLIN. But you see? You shouldn't have to. Maybe if you were with someone else and he kissed you, you'd be knocked off your feet and unable to think about anything else.

MONICA. I don't want anyone else. All I have to do is let go more. I keep such a tight grip on everything in case –

COLIN. In case of what?

MONICA. There's so many things to take care of.

COLIN. What about Monica? Don't you need to be taken care of, too? *(He crosses to the desk area and with a cloth wipes off a big chunk of writing on the planning board.)* You have all these deadly deadlines and they're all so important to you. But what are they really? Is the country going to collapse if "bio and pic due Fri" is late? Will the world stop if Suzi doesn't have her photo session on the twenty-second? Monica, you live by all these self-imposed deadlines, yet you've ignored your own.

MONICA. *(beat)* God. I love you like this. You're worried about me.

COLIN. *(firmly)* No. I'm saying *I*, me, Colin, I want you all there when I'm making love to you. That's purely selfish and not too much to ask.

MONICA. No. It's the perfect thing to ask.

COLIN. Sorry.

MONICA. It's this room. Even though I turn off the bells, I can hear a little rat-a-tat-tat every time the phone rings.

COLIN. How about if we go to my place?

MONICA. After the opening?

COLIN. After.

MONICA. I'll fix you breakfast on the beach.

COLIN. You're planning.

MONICA. Right. We'll play tomorrow's morning meal by ear.

COLIN. Yeah. *(He stares at her.)*

MONICA. What?

*(**COLIN** kisses her passionately. They sink to the floor. **MONICA** starts unbuttoning his shirt. They roll around in an embrace and gently knock tables and furniture.)*

*(**COLIN** & **MONICA**'s kiss is interrupted by a blood-curdling scream offstage. They break and stand, both in various states of undress.)*

MONICA. I'll get my mace.

AMANDA. *(offstage)* I can't believe it! Monica! I have a life! *(another scream.)*

(**ERROL** *and* **AMANDA** *enter with champagne and see* **COLIN** *and* **MONICA** *coming at them still undressed.*)

ERROL. Oops. Looks like we interrupted a post-dinner discussion.

AMANDA. Negative! The test was negative!

MONICA. How do you know?

COLIN. That's great.

MONICA. I thought you wouldn't get the results until tomorrow?

AMANDA. I called Dr. Keltnor and he said he had heard from the lab sooner than he expected so I quantum leaped to his office.

COLIN. And it's negative? They're positive? I mean –

AMANDA. Yes! *(She screams again.)*

(**JEANNETTE** *dances in her chiffon nightgown. Her hair is down and the nightgown billows as she dances.*)

(in tears) Mom?

(**JEANNETTE** *dances over to* **AMANDA** *and tries to touch her. She is concerned because* **AMANDA** *screamed.*)

AMANDA. Mom, Dr. Keltnor told me I won't get Huntington's.

(**JEANNETTE** *is stunned. She tries to speak. She indicates for* **AMANDA** *to repeat.*)

Yes, you heard right. You didn't pass it on, Mom.

(**JEANNETTE** *waltzes around gleefully. She smiles at all and stops at* **MONICA** *realizing the awkward position* **MONICA** *is now in.*)

AMANDA. *(beat, then to* **MONICA**) Thank you. I know it wasn't –

MONICA. Oh, forget it. It's not like I donated a kidney or anything.

AMANDA. That would have been easier. I wish I could tell you how it feels.

MONICA. That's coming across loud and clear. *(She crosses to the planning board and fills in where* **COLIN** *erased.)*

AMANDA. I feel...I feel...like I was one of those old ladies with a curved spine and it just went straight! Really. Do I look taller?

*(***HANK** *enters in underwear and a Hawaiian shirt.)*

HANK. What's all the ruckus?

AMANDA. Daddy, the test was negative. I...don't...I won't get Huntington's!

HANK. Really? Oh, that's...the best news, Mandy. *(looking around)* Nettie?

*(***JEANNETTE** *takes the phone to* **MONICA**, *breaking the cord in the process. She drops the phone in* **MONICA**'s *lap.)*

MONICA. Mother, I can't. They don't just tell you. You have to go through counseling and...I can't. You said you wouldn't have been able to either, remember?

*(***JEANNETTE** *dances away.)*

Remember?!

*(***JEANNETTE** *dances out.)*

AMANDA. Let's go out! I want to seriously celebrate and try and thank you for –

MONICA. No. You go and enjoy your...news.

AMANDA. But I'd want you there.

MONICA. No you wouldn't. I'd be a downer and you need to be up. I'll bring you down later.

ERROL. Let's go to the mountains!

MONICA. Really. Revel however you want.

AMANDA. The mountains? Yes! I want to see the sunrise tomorrow. I want a glorious start to the rest of my life.

ERROL. Now, hold the phone here. You've been stringing this out for two weeks now saying, "it's just one long date." Will this count as a second?

AMANDA. No. Because I'm a new person.

ERROL. Does this new girl go out on second dates?

AMANDA. I don't know her that well. *(They start to exit.)* "Girl?" Don't you love him? *(at the door)* Monica, you sure?

(MONICA nods. AMANDA rushes over, embraces MONICA and runs out. They exit.)

HANK. *(to MONICA)* You still don't want to start the counseling so you could – ?

MONICA. I couldn't handle getting the grade, Daddy. Would you have wanted to know when Momma was thirty-six?

HANK. *(after a beat)* No. *(He exits.)*

COLIN. Let me get you a drink; a serious drink.

MONICA. I can't – ! *(She stops herself, then covers.)* I can't stomach the thought. *(beat)* I don't know how she did it. I would have snapped. I would have gone completely berserk between the actual test and getting the results.

COLIN. If I went with you to the counseling, would you consider – ?

MONICA. Why are you so anxious for me to take this test?

COLIN. So you can get –

MONICA. Isn't it for you? So you can know whether it's worth it to continue this relationship?

COLIN. No. Monica. It's not…for me.

MONICA. *(beat)* So, you're wearing that tonight?

COLIN. I'll go see if I have anything in your closet that might be God-daughter-meeting-presentable-enough."

MONICA. Uh-oh.

COLIN. You threw them out in a fit of rage?

MONICA. I'll heat up the iron. You look under the shoes.

(JEANNETTE dances in as COLIN and MONICA kiss lightly. He exits. JEANNETTE dances to a phone and tries to pick it up.)

MONICA. Mom, I don't want to know.

(JEANNETTE is emphatic with the phone. MONICA takes it from her and replaces it. She takes both of JEANNETTE's hands in hers which steadies JEANNETTE somewhat.)

MONICA. Mom. I haven't told this to anyone yet. I'm not totally sure either and I debated if I should tell Colin first or Mandy or anyone. I should go to the doctor before I say anything, but I know. You just know.
And then, tonight when I saw your face light up with Mandy's news, I knew I had to tell you. Mom, it's time for a grandchild.

(JEANNETTE starts to struggle. JEANNETTE breaks away and dances all around the room in joyful abandon, even emitting little noises. MONICA watches her with tears in her eyes, then JEANNETTE picks up COLIN's jacket and smells it. Then, she shows it to MONICA.)

MONICA. Yes. Colin is the father. I'm going to tell him now.

(JEANNETTE looks back at MONICA and runs to her and tries to embrace her, then goes back to the phone.)

MONICA. I know. I know. You want me to get the results. But I can't, Mother. I want this baby.

(JEANNETTE dances with COLIN's coat. MONICA crosses upstage behind the same parachute silk divider JEANNETTE appeared behind at the top of the act.)

(Lights go to half. We see MONICA standing in silhouette behind the silk. COLIN approaches her. We see that she tells him her news. He is shocked at first, but then embraces her.)

(JEANNETTE drops the jacket. She faces the audience. Tears fill her eyes. Her arms, now at her side, begin to tremble. Gradually, the trembling overtakes her entire torso. She tries to reach out to the audience to tell us something. She tries, shaking more violently every second. Her head shakes uncontrollably. Her fingers involuntarily thump her chest repeatedly as the lights fade.)

(Curtain act one)

ACT TWO

Scene One

(SCENE: Six weeks later. Late morning.)

*(**MONICA** is seated at the switchboard. **HANK** is folding stacks of paper and stuffing envelopes.)*

MONICA. *(into phone)* It's a satellite broadcast for "Good Morning Australia." His call is at 2:30 PM with live bounce at 2:45…Yeah. It's great; that's the first hour of GMA, so it's the best…That's perfect. Let him sleep right up till the broadcast. It'll be early in Australia and if he looks like he just got up, he'll match…Yeah. Gotta go; line 3 and 4 are waiting. *(She switches lines.)* Grapevine, thanks for holding.

*(**AMANDA** enters in a kimono and sits at switchboard with a cup of coffee. During the following phone conversations, **JEANNETTE** dances in carrying two large bundles of mail. She wears a small "walkman" cassette player around her waist and small headphones around her neck. She releases the mail in a flurry all over the room. She continues dancing. Without missing a beat, **HANK** starts collecting and sorting the mail.)*

MONICA.

(into phone) What do you mean he canceled? I have had these interviews set up for weeks. I can't go back to major dailies and tell them nada interviews.
……………………
…………….. Uh huh. Right…Fine…Bye.
(She hangs up)

AMANDA.

(into phone) Grapevine… Yes. He absolutely insists the pictures have to be touched up…I know it costs a fortune…We can't use the old ones. It's totally forbidden. They're pre-nose job…I don't know. He's sensitive, remember? Okay…… Right…Fine… Bye.
(She hangs up)

AMANDA. Anything good, Daddy?
HANK. Lotta bills, press releases.
MONICA. Any checks?
HANK. Yep. Looks like it.

(**HANK** *holds up a few envelopes that appear to have checks in them.* **JEANNETTE** *takes them from him and dances with them.*)

HANK. Mommy always loved when the mail came.
MONICA. She loves the checks.
AMANDA. She sure seems happy lately. Is she on some new drug?
MONICA. No. I think she's just happy for you, Mandy. It must be quite a relief for her.
AMANDA. *(to* **MONICA***)* And you seem gloomier than ever.
MONICA. Well, sorry I can't be sickeningly chipper like you.
AMANDA. I'm not chipper!
MONICA. Why not? You have every right to be.
AMANDA. What's on today?
MONICA. We had phoners for Mac, but he flaked.
AMANDA. Again?
MONICA. And we have a screening at two and a sneak at eight.
AMANDA. Who do I talk to about a vacation?
HANK. Vacation? What's that?
AMANDA. When you go to a travel agent and give them a departure date and destination, you buy traveller's checks, lots of those little travel containers and you're gone for a couple of months.

(**JEANNETTE** *shakes her head violently.*)

MONICA. Months? What happened to two weeks?
AMANDA. Well, I've never had a vacation, so I figure I have a good six months coming. You, too.
MONICA. Oh. So we should just put a "gone fishing" message on the exchange and close for half a year?
AMANDA. No. I'll train a temp.
MONICA. Dad? What do you think?

HANK. Sounds more than fair. Nettie?

(**JEANNETTE** *shakes her head and dances to* **AMANDA** *to plead with her.*)

AMANDA. Mom. Don't worry. The place won't fall apart if I'm gone a while.

MONICA. Turn off the bell. Dad, can you watch the phones? If they all light up, call us.

HANK. Will do.

(**MONICA** *kisses* **HANK** *and she and* **AMANDA** *cross to another area.* **JEANNETTE** *follows them, dancing.*)

MONICA. How soon do you want to go?

AMANDA. I'm not asking permission, understand Sis?

MONICA. Yes. No, we've always been equal. It's just that *we* need you here now.

AMANDA. Oh. You'd say that any week.

MONICA. Yeah. But I'd mean it this month. I'm *in* my third month.

AMANDA. Of?

MONICA. Bunning in the oven.

AMANDA. Sure.

MONICA. Truth.

AMANDA. You are fucking kidding me.

(**JEANNETTE** *shakes her head violently.*)

MONICA. No.

AMANDA. No? This isn't some hideous, distasteful, perverted excuse to keep me from –

MONICA. Give me credit.

AMANDA. I do! It'd work and you'd stop at – Whoah! You and Colin? It's his baby – He – *(She stops.)* It *is* his baby, isn't it?

MONICA. Unless one of your strays drifted in my room and made a quick night deposit, it's his.

AMANDA. He knows? (**MONICA** *nods.*) Really? This is – Oh. No way!

(**AMANDA** *embraces* **MONICA**, **JEANNETTE** *tries to embrace them too. Then* **AMANDA** *backs away.*)

AMANDA. You asshole!

MONICA. What?

AMANDA. Why didn't you tell me? I'm your goddam sister, business partner – I thought, friend. Why didn't I notice? How self-centered of me.

MONICA. I haven't exactly been broadcasting.

AMANDA. What about all those lectures you gave me about condoms and now –

MONICA. Hey, I'm not a frequent flyer like you. We were doubly cautious at first, then I just trusted my diaphragm.

AMANDA. But, Monica, he travels all over the world.

MONICA. He's not – *(She stops).* All right, I was irresponsible.

(JEANNETTE dances away from the girls.)

AMANDA. So, two months ago, when I asked you if you were…you were.

MONICA. Yes.

AMANDA. Monica, you –

MONICA. It's too late. I'm going through with this pregnancy.

AMANDA. What does Colin have to say about all this?

MONICA. He's being disgustingly supportive and committed. I wasn't going to tell him.

AMANDA. You weren't going to tell me either? What did you plan to do? Go have this baby in a rice field and then hide it for twenty years?

MONICA. I just told Mother first. I was going to tell you as soon as –

AMANDA. That's why she's been so happy. But she must –

MONICA. She understands completely, even to the point that she's putting pressure on me to go in and –

AMANDA. Evidently not enough. What did Colin say when you told him?

MONICA. He still wants to move in together.

(JEANNETTE dances over to MONICA and appears to applaud.)

MONICA. There's this nagging thing in me that says he doesn't really love me; he's just going out of his way to *prove* he won't run out.

AMANDA. You have no self respect. Why couldn't you be entitled to have a wonderful man adore you?

MONICA. An ace in my crummy hand?

AMANDA. Just stop, will you? *(beat)* God, Nicky. It still hasn't sunk in. A baby.

(**JEANNETTE** *tries to feel* **MONICA**'s *stomach and in the process inadvertently knocks* **MONICA**'s *stomach.*)

AMANDA. Mother!

MONICA. It's okay. She just wants to feel the baby.

AMANDA. You can't feel it yet.

MONICA. Flutters. We tape recorded the baby's heartbeat and I let Mom hear it on the walkman.

AMANDA. *That's* what that was. She wanted me to rewind it and I listened and I thought one of her books-on-tape was defective.

(**JEANNETTE** *tries to take* **AMANDA**'s *hand and place it on* **MONICA**'s *stomach.*)

AMANDA. What does she want?

MONICA. She wants you to feel.

(**MONICA** *takes* **AMANDA**'s *hand and places it on her stomach.* **JEANNETTE** *dances around the room.*)

MONICA. She was a mother. She remembers.

AMANDA. It's like you swallowed an eggplant whole.

MONICA. Sometimes it seems like that inside.

AMANDA. I suppose you've told Dad?

HANK. Yes. But I'm sworn to secrecy.

AMANDA. How come you didn't tell me sooner? I feel like odd-man out.

MONICA. Don't. I…just thought you'd try and –

AMANDA. Talk you into abortion? I couldn't. But the one thing I will not stop at is you getting those results. I won't sleep until you do.

MONICA. Better get the espresso machine fixed.

AMANDA. Do you mean, if I hadn't asked about a vacation, you wouldn't have said anything?

MONICA. It will be obvious in a few weeks. Yes. Take your vacation immediately so you can relieve me when the baby comes.

AMANDA. No. I'll postpone my trip to get you through the test.

MONICA. Mandy, I am going to love being pregnant. I'll only do it once. I don't want to spoil it with bad test results.

AMANDA. You're impossible.

MONICA. Yep.

AMANDA. Do you think I could coerce Colin into taking my passport picture?

MONICA. Sure.

AMANDA. He could take yours, too.

MONICA. That would be futile.

HANK. They're all lit up!

AMANDA. We should get back.

MONICA. If anything happens, I want you to be the guardian.

AMANDA. Me? Irresponsible little sister?

MONICA. I've asked everyone else and they turned me down.

AMANDA. No. You didn't ask anyone, did you? Especially not me. And I'm the one who'll…

MONICA. Take good care.

*(Light fade to half. **JEANNETTE** begins to shake and tremble. She picks up a pale lipstick that **AMANDA** left on a table and crosses downstage to an imaginary mirror. She tries to apply the lipstick, but it goes all over her face because of the trembling. She smooths her hips and notices the tape player. She takes the headphones from around her neck and holds them next to her heart, pleased that there's a fetal heartbeat. She exits as lights up from half to full.)*

(It is now:)

Scene Two

(SCENE: One month later. Late morning.)

(AMANDA is seated at the desk. ERROL is doing sit-ups on the floor. AMANDA is looking at a page of slides, holding them up to the light and occasionally removing one.)

ERROL. I thought I'd just meet you in Paris.

AMANDA. Oh. So you can't get two weeks off?

ERROL. No. I'll get a cheapie flight and join you for one week.

AMANDA. You don't have to join me at all.

ERROL. I know.

AMANDA. And if you haven't already gotten a cheap flight, you're not going to. The idea is to buy months ahead.

ERROL. Oh.

AMANDA. You knew that. Errol, let me make this real easy for you. Stay home.

ERROL. No. I want to go. Really, I do.

AMANDA. Bullshit. You're going to be a terrible agent. You have to be able to lie a lot more convincingly.

ERROL. Well, I have been kind of hemming and hawing.

AMANDA. Did you think I wouldn't notice?

ERROL. There's an assistantship coming up in three weeks and I feel they're watching us. So, it'd be better for me if –

AMANDA. Then, it's settled. You have to stay.

ERROL. You sound relieved.

AMANDA. I am. Don't look so disappointed. You made me break my rule. You've achieved a major conquest.

ERROL. But when you reduce it down to rules and conquests, it sounds so stupid.

AMANDA. I know. That's why I don't do second dates. There's no need to discuss anything.

ERROL. But, I thought you thought I was funny.

AMANDA. You are. But I'm just too old for you and too plain.

ERROL. Don't say that. You're not plain.

AMANDA. The only reason you approached and dueled was because of the challenge. You had to prove something. And you did. I chose not to tell anyone about my possible middle-aged need to jitterbug twenty-four hours a day and that…made me interesting. Now that that's gone. I'm just another drab thirty-year-old broad lusting after your body.

ERROL. Are you saying you want to call it quits?

AMANDA. Considering I never wanted to call it starts, yes.

ERROL. Am I being dumped?

AMANDA. No, precious. That will never happen. I'm giving you permission to dump me. Because now I want a stable relationship with someone a little older, with possibly a little less hair and maybe a little fat on his stomach.

ERROL. Really? Have I been doing 1,000 sit-ups a day for nothing?

AMANDA. Probably.

ERROL. You're pulling my leg.

AMANDA. No. I'm through pulling anything of yours, Err, babe. You're going to be an agent. You'll need a very young, very vivacious wife or none at all.

ERROL. So, you'll go to Europe all by yourself?

AMANDA. Yes. And I will love it. I've never had privacy, ever. Can you imagine? Never.

ERROL. Is this like another challenge, another hurdle for me?

AMANDA. You've dumped me. I've survived. Weren't you supposed to be delivering something and won't they be missing you?

ERROL. Yeah.

AMANDA. You'll miss your chance to be spotted for the assistantship.

ERROL. That lady never comes in this early.

AMANDA. Lady, huh?

ERROL. *(smiles)* Yeah.

AMANDA. Wear the tight khaki.

ERROL. You think?

AMANDA. Kill.

ERROL. Okay. I'll go then.

AMANDA. Yes. You're a gentle dumper.

ERROL. Thanks. *(He kisses her.)* You want a poke for the road?

AMANDA. No. Errol save your erections. You only get 20,000.

ERROL. What?

AMANDA. It's a proven fact. And in California, there's so much pollution and chlorine in the water, the number is even smaller.

ERROL. You're putting me on.

AMANDA. Do you want me to show you in my medical dictionary?

ERROL. Does that include at night when you dream and you – ?

AMANDA. Absolutely.

ERROL. Shit. 20,000? Let's see. 365 days a year times…Say, four. God.

*(**AMANDA** can't contain her laughter.)*

ERROL. I'll kill you.

AMANDA. I read it somewhere. Honest. My point is: for whatever reason, use them sparingly.

ERROL. Okay. *(He starts to exit.)* Can I still get tickets to Mac's next concert?

AMANDA. A promise is a promise.

ERROL. But you'll be in Europe.

*(**MONICA & COLIN** enter carrying baby-name books and eating carrot sticks.)*

MONICA. How about "Robert Louis?"

COLIN. What makes you think we'll have a male poet?

MONICA. A feeling. Or "Byron?"

AMANDA. Monica will cover you.

MONICA. With what?

AMANDA. Mac tickets.

MONICA. Oh. You're not going to Europe together?

ERROL. We're not going anywhere together.

AMANDA. We're not going together.

COLIN. So much for dates #39, 40 and 41.

MONICA. *(to* **ERROL***)* What are you doing with your plane ticket?

AMANDA. He never bought it.

ERROL. Yeah. So, if I call up in three weeks and ask for Mac tickets, you'll remember me, right?

MONICA. We'll never forget you.

ERROL. God, I can't believe me. I'm such an opportunist. I dump Amanda and three minutes later, I ask her sister for free tickets.

MONICA. At least you recognize the fact that you have no scruples. There's hope for you. It's the people who don't see that in themselves we have to watch out for.

ERROL. Right. Yeah.

AMANDA. *(looking away, masking her pained attraction to* **ERROL***)* Hit the road, Err. You're supposed to dump and leave, not loiter.

ERROL. Okay. Bye. I'm sure I'll see you around.

AMANDA. Bye, cutie.

*(***ERROL** *exits.)*

AMANDA. I thought he'd never leave.

MONICA. What happened to going to Europe together?

AMANDA. Did you really think we would?

HANK. *(offstage)* Nicky?!

MONICA. Yeah?

HANK. It's that lady from "20/20" on your private line.

MONICA. Oh, God. The bells are still off. *(She exits.)*

AMANDA. Back to work. *(She heads for the desk.)*

COLIN. Hey. Are you all right?

AMANDA. Oh, sure. I'll miss him, but really. Who am I kidding?

COLIN. It seemed comfortable…fun.

AMANDA. I actually liked going out with the same guy for six weeks. I'd played the field so long there wasn't any astroturf left. And right now it's kinda hip for him to be seen with an older woman. But how long will that last? As the crows feet creep in, that "coolness" will wear off.

COLIN. Not necessarily if you –

MONICA. *(offstage)* Yes! Yes! Yes! *(She enters.)* Ooh, I'm good!!

AMANDA. What miracle did you pull off now?

MONICA. "20/20" is going to cover the benefit.

AMANDA. Really?

MONICA. They're planning a piece on saving trees in the Brasilian and Hawaiian rainforests and this will fit in perfectly.

COLIN. *(looking at the book again)* How about Coleen?

MONICA. Colin/Coleen? Cute. I feel left out already.

AMANDA. I have to go pick up some the benefit invitations. Excuse me if I don't participate in the great-name-the-baby-debate. *(She starts to exit.)*

MONICA. You ordered recycled paper, didn't you?

AMANDA. You're slipping, Nick. Not only did you ask me before, but you called the printers to make sure.

MONICA. Right.

*(**AMANDA** exits. **MONICA** sits next to **COLIN** and closes his baby name book.)*

COLIN. I'm tired of looking at names, too.

MONICA. Dylan?

COLIN. Sold!

MONICA. Really?

COLIN. Yeah. Can we elope now?

MONICA. I'm ready, but are you? You keep bringing this up so I assume you're serious.

COLIN. Dead.

MONICA. Yes. That's exactly it. I feel like I'll be killing you; like you've accepted this death sentence and you want to get it over with.

COLIN. No. You're not.

MONICA. I feel horrible tying you down.

COLIN. Don't. It's a commitment, that's all. And I need to make it.

MONICA. Do we really have to get married?

COLIN. Yes.

MONICA. Why?

COLIN. I want to feel like we're a family when we become one.

MONICA. And a little piece of paper will do that for you?

COLIN. I come from a family of lawyers. Little pieces of paper with names and signatures make us happy.

MONICA. I can't marry you and say, "Till death do us part" and mean it. Especially if I turn into a quivering –

COLIN. Don't say it.

MONICA. Why not? I'd marry you if you promised me you'd kill me if I got the dance of death.

(beat)

COLIN. How can you say that?

MONICA. Would you?

COLIN. If I promised to kill you, would you marry me? My God. What am I saying? Did I just hear me?

(JEANNETTE enters pushing a stroller filled with pictures in frames. She pushes the stroller into MONICA.)

COLIN. Hi, Mrs. G.

(JEANNETTE drifts away from COLIN and indicates she wants MONICA to look in the stroller.)

MONICA. Mom, these are pictures of you, you and Daddy, you and me and Mandy.

COLIN. Did you want me to see pictures of when the girls were little?

(**JEANNETTE** *shakes her head and dances over to* **MONICA** *and drops shredded photographs in her lap. Then she dances away.*)

MONICA. What did you do? (*She looks at the pictures.*) This is from Daddy's birthday party last year. Why would you tear these up? And this – ? (*She stops*). Mother, you only want the baby to see pictures of you before you got sick?

(*No evident reaction from* **JEANNETTE**.)

MONICA. But Mother, the baby will know you. He'll be fascinated by you. He won't have any preconceived images of a grandma. He'll accept you and love you.

(**JEANNETTE** *shakes her head violently, then dances out.*)

COLIN. She's amazing.

MONICA. You should have seen her fifteen years ago. She was the epitome of elegance. She always wore hats. Now they don't stay…

COLIN. I couldn't. I couldn't make that promise.

MONICA. Well, then, I'll take care of it myself. If I get it, I'll –

COLIN. You keep saying that. How can you stand it? Wouldn't you at least like one "if" out of your life?

MONICA. If I get it, I'll have to kill myself early while I'm still lucid.

COLIN. Monica. This is sick to talk like this.

MONICA. No, it's not. It's real. It's a sickness, yes. And I'm doing the best I can to try and deal –

COLIN. We'll deal with it later. Just don't make it a condition of marriage.

MONICA. Very well. I'll withdraw it.

COLIN. And you may not get it.

MONICA. *(beat)* Promise this: that you'll remember my wishes? I don't want to be a burden or institutionalized. And promise me that if I am unable to speak – for whatever reason – and you look in my eyes, that you'll know and you'll remember and you'll do something.

COLIN. I promise I'll remember your wishes.

MONICA. Thank you.

COLIN. So. Can we get one of those little pieces of paper with signatures over it and your name and mine?

MONICA. If that's what you want.

COLIN. I do. And you do, too?

MONICA. I do.

COLIN. There. See? We both said "I do" and did it feel like twenty-seven canker sores? *(They kiss.)*

MONICA. But you can't go on long foreign junkets, okay? Because we may have to squeeze fifty years into ten and that won't work if you're never here.

COLIN. Deal. *(He reaches into his duffel bag and pulls out a Chinese food take-out box.)* Here.

MONICA. What's this?

COLIN. I've been eating a lot of Chinese food and –

MONICA. Chow Mein for breakfast? *(She opens the box. It has one fortune cookie in it. She cracks open the fortune cookie. There is an engagement ring in it.)*

COLIN. One picture worth thousand words.

MONICA. This isn't the ring you put a deposit on for the lady that got the CD consolation prize?

COLIN. No.

MONICA. When did you do this?

COLIN. Couple of weeks ago. I wanted to be prepared in case *you* asked.

MONICA. Does this mean I won't get a portable CD player?

COLIN. Yes.

*(**MONICA** puts the ring on her finger and holds it up to the light. They kiss. **HANK** enters excitedly. He stops when he sees them kissing. He watches for a beat, then clears his throat. They break.)*

HANK. Sorry to…I wouldn't normally interrupt, but it's the White House.

MONICA. No shit.

HANK. That's what they said; the Press Secretary's Office.

MONICA. Oh, my God. *(to* **COLIN***)* Hold that kiss. *(She exits.)*

HANK. Have you seen Nettie?

COLIN. Yeah. She just came through here.

HANK. It's time for her bath.

COLIN. Bath?

HANK. Well, shower. But we do it in the tub. We have one of those sprayer things, you know?

COLIN. You "do it" together?

HANK. Oh, yeah. It makes it seem less like you're cleaning an invalid, see.

COLIN. And it's sexy, too.

HANK. Sometimes…not usually. Maybe I'm getting too old.

COLIN. Nah.

HANK. *(beat)* Actually, what I told the kid a while back, that was – well, bragging. I wanted to shock him. Probably would have shocked him even more if I'd told him the truth.

COLIN. You mean about having sex with Jeannette?

HANK. Yeah. It's not…like…It's like trying to clap with one hand.

COLIN. Oh.

HANK. I just didn't want you to have the wrong impression.

*(***JEANNETTE*** waltzes in.)*

HANK. There you are. Ready for our shower, Mommy?

*(***JEANNETTE*** waltzes up to* **HANK***, ready to follow.)*

COLIN. Hank, could you maybe get the water warm and give us a minute?

HANK. Sure. *(as he exits)* Wonder if we have any Vitabath left?

COLIN. Jeannette, if you Glendenning-Girls are really such intense planners, how can you allow Monica to live with this big question?

(JEANNETTE *waltzes away and begins her hit herself.*
COLIN *stops her and tries to hold her arms.*)

COLIN. I could never tell her this, but I'm frightened of not knowing. And I think, ultimately, that she'd regret not learning the results sooner.

(JEANNETTE *waltzes in place, staring at him.*)

Hank's waiting.

(JEANNETTE *moves closer to* COLIN *and tries to stroke his hand, but can't. She exits almost colliding with re-entering* MONICA.)

MONICA. Careful, Mom.

COLIN. Well what's the good word from the Oval Office?

MONICA. "Oh. What a wonderful cause. Keep up the good work." Neither Prez nor Vice-Prez can fit us in, but they'll send a telegram we can read out loud if we supply a suggested sample of what we'd like them to say! Can you believe that?

Now where were we?

COLIN. You put our lips on hold, remember?

MONICA. Oh, yes. Are you sick of Chinese? We could order –

COLIN. Oh, my God. You're gonna hate me...more. I just remembered I have a session in Hollywood in an hour.

(*He kisses her, grabs his bag and starts to exit nearly colliding with* AMANDA *who is returning with a box from the printer.*)

MONICA. When will you be back?

COLIN. I don't know. It's an all-girl group and you know how they are.

MONICA. Yes. They'll take you out to dinner and I'm already jealous.

COLIN. *(as he exits)* I'll call you from the studio.

MONICA. Like hell. *(She slips the ring into her pocket.)*

COLIN. *(offstage)* I will.

AMANDA. Fresh off the presses, madame. Your recycled invites.

MONICA. Let me see. Let me see. How'd they turn out?

AMANDA. Perfect.

*(**MONICA** opens a box before **AMANDA** even has a chance to set them down.)*

AMANDA. They apologized for being late. The recycled paper didn't take the colors too well and –

MONICA. They're not late. I told them a day ahead of time. If you got this in the mail, wouldn't you be inclined to buy a table? *(She picks up phone. Then to **AMANDA**)* Hungry? I was going to order in Thai.

AMANDA. I'll bring some back.

MONICA. Oh. Errands?

AMANDA. I'm going shopping.

MONICA. But today's invoicing. You love invoicing.

AMANDA. "Love?" Well, let's say, that of all my slave chores, it's the least hateful. I just got off on sending some arrogant rock star or movie idol a huge bill for keeping them in or out of the limelight. It can wait.

MONICA. What are you shopping for?

AMANDA. Things to take on my trip; luggage to put those things in.

MONICA. Want company?

AMANDA. No. I…well…

MONICA. It's okay.

AMANDA. Nicky, I spend all day, everyday, here with you. We live under the same roof. I just need some solitude.

MONICA. Sure.

AMANDA. Leave the invoicing. We'll do it tonight. *(She starts to exit.)*

MONICA. You seem distant.

AMANDA. Yeah? Well, my mind is on my trip.

MONICA. No. At work last week, this week, before…

AMANDA. So? Fire me!

MONICA. I'm serious. You let those radio I.D.'s slip by, the press packets went out late –

AMANDA. You want me to quit? I will.

MONICA. No. That's the last thing I'd want.

AMANDA. That's for sure. You'd have to pay somebody a lot of money to do what I do.

MONICA. Yes.

AMANDA. Who gave you the authority to review my job performance?

*(**AMANDA** starts to exit. **MONICA** stops her. **AMANDA** struggles free.)*

AMANDA. Let me go.

MONICA. You're going on vacation. Isn't that enough?

AMANDA. No. They just issued me extra pages in my passport. And I intend to fill them.

MONICA. Good for you! But what you do mean, "Let me go?" What's happened to us, Mandy? A few weeks ago –

AMANDA. Only little things have happened, Nick: I took a test and found out I have a life, you got yourself knocked up and insist on remaining in the dark.

MONICA. So? It's all my fault for not going through with –

AMANDA. You are carrying a child that could be faced with the same life we've had. If you had any guts you'd learn the results and deal with it. It's not fair to the baby –

MONICA. What about me!?

AMANDA. What about you?

MONICA. *(beat)* Okay. I'm scared. I'm terrified of being alone. A month ago, you and I were in the same boat. It wasn't necessarily a great ride, but we were in it together. Then you rocked the boat by being so goddam brave. I'm alone in here. *(beat)* And I want a baby, a family. Is that so terrible?

AMANDA. I just want you to think of the baby.

MONICA. I do. Constantly.

AMANDA. Would you wish your life on a child?

MONICA. Yes. Until Mother got sick, it was pretty decent. And since then, it's been up and down, but mostly up.

AMANDA. Then, no doubt you've considered that your child will not have the same luxury of ignorance that we did. He will know that this disease is a possible factor in his life. He'll have that question staring him in the face much sooner – and longer – than we did. Oh, what's the use? Nothing I say ever has an effect on you. I'll never change your mind.

MONICA. I change fifty times a day. If the seed has been passed on, then I will just have to have every faith that they'll come up with a cure in the next forty-six years. Go shop.

(**JEANNETTE** *dances in carrying a rattle. She dances over to* **AMANDA**.)

AMANDA. Really. Leave the invoices.

(**JEANNETTE** *pulls on* **AMANDA**'s *shirt sleeve and motions her to do something.*)

MONICA. I will.

HANK. *(offstage)* Nettie.

AMANDA. Mother, do you need something? Nicky? What's…?

MONICA. I don't know.

(**HANK** *enters wearing a terrycloth robe.*)

HANK. Nettie, come on, doll. Let's hit the shower.

(**JEANNETTE** *shakes her head, "No."*)

HANK. What's the matter? This isn't like you.

AMANDA. She hasn't been herself lately, Daddy.

HANK. I know. Something's eating at her. Okay. Nettie, I'm going to go shave. Then you be ready in five. I'm not getting dressed, then undressed again.

MONICA. I'll bring her in, Dad.

HANK. Pronto. Or I'm comin' at her with a hose. *(He exits.)*

AMANDA. It's very strange. *(She looks at* **JEANNETTE**.*)* This morning I was putting on my mascara and I caught a glimpse of Mom in the mirror trying to watch me.

And I remembered that one of the things I dreaded about getting Huntington's was that I wouldn't be able to wear make-up. Isn't that the stupidest? I saw her watch me and remembered how she prided herself on her appearance. *(beat)* And so, I looked at myself today in that mirror and I said, "Who are you? You've postponed your life so long, you don't have one."

MONICA. Is this supposed to make me feel better?

AMANDA. No. Oddly enough, everything I say is not intended to cheer *you* up. I'm just saying that I have no gameplan.

MONICA. So, develop one in Europe and stop feeling sorry for yourself. You, thank God, will be able to wear make-up till the day you die.

(JEANNETTE *pushes* AMANDA.)

AMANDA. Do you want to show me something?

(JEANNETTE *shakes her head.*)

MONICA. I think she wants to show *me* something.

(JEANNETTE *stops, then resumes a subdued dance.*)

AMANDA. I can take a hint. Did you want to go shopping?

MONICA. No. You go. Enjoy. I going to seriously browse through my catalogues of baby furniture.

AMANDA. It's just a kid. Throw it in a drawer. *(She exits.)*

(JEANNETTE *goes to large wall calendar and hits it.*)

MONICA. What is it, Mom? An important date?

(JEANNETTE *shakes her head and dances to the phone and picks it up and drops the receiver.*)

MONICA. No, Mom. I can't do what Mandy did. You have to understand. There are limits to the things I can face right now.

(JEANNETTE *takes the rattle and repeatedly whacks it on the calendar. She drops the rattle and gets frustrated. She knocks over the pens. She swats the pens so they fly to the calendar and picks up the phone and throws it at* MONICA.)

MONICA. Mother, stop! Please. It's too much. Go slow. Rattle? Baby? Planner? *(beat)*

(**JEANNETTE** *knows that* **MONICA** *understands now and dances calmly.*)

MONICA. You want me to take the test so I can plan for the baby.

(**JEANNETTE** *shakes her head. She gestures to her throat and then to the rattle.*)

MONICA. So I can *tell* the baby. But I thought you said you couldn't have taken it either. (**JEANNETTE** *shakes her head. Beat.*) You think I have it, don't you?

(**JEANNETTE** *shakes her head and dances away from* **MONICA**, *hitting her head with her hands.*)

MONICA. I wish you could drive me, Mom, like you used to take me to the dermatologist, the orthodontist. You always took such great care of us. You still do.

(**JEANNETTE** *dances to* **MONICA** *and throws herself at* **MONICA***'s feet.* **MONICA** *stands numb.*)

MONICA. Mom, this is very difficult. Going through with this test would be – I thought you understood that better than anyone. *(She kneels down and raises* **JEANNETTE***).* I guess you do. I…I can't, Mom. Not now.

(Lights fade to half as **MONICA** *exits.)*

(**JEANNETTE** *begins to shake and tremble. She moves the stroller almost offstage. She removes a baby doll and holds it professionally, cradling the head in her hand. She looks lovingly at the baby, then embraces the baby in one hand while pushing the stoller off with her other hand.*)

(Lights up to full)

(It is now:)

Scene Three

(SCENE: Six weeks later. Dusk.)

(Luggage is stacked near the entrance. A "Bon Voyage" banner is hung across the room. **HANK & COLIN** *pick up confetti and streamers.)*

HANK. Nicky sure knows how to throw a helluva party.

COLIN. Yep.

HANK. Course, she gets that from her mom. Nettie would have probably insisted it be at a hotel though. She didn't like anyone to be put out. People know where a hotel is, they don't have to look it up on a map or get lost. There's parking, whatever they want to drink, plenty of bathrooms.

COLIN. Well, Monica's great at planning parties, but she was useless today.

HANK. That'd happen to Nettie too, sometimes.

(MONICA enters looking slightly more pregnant and flushed.)

MONICA. Oh, you guys don't have to do that.

HANK. Somebody's got to. *(He continues cleaning.)*

COLIN. You sure look pretty today.

MONICA. Do you always have to say the right thing?

COLIN. Sorry. Actually I was going to say radiant. Would that have been wronger?

MONICA. Yes. Because we both know I wasn't. I was a knocked up wallflower.

COLIN. You're entitled.

MONICA. Too supportive.

COLIN. What do you want me to say?

MONICA. I don't know.

COLIN. Something cruel so you can get mad, so you can get emotional?

MONICA. Oh, I'm having no problem getting that.

COLIN. So, what happened today? You got to see all those people you haven't seen in months and –

MONICA. All I could see was the new luggage. It's never been anywhere and it's going everywhere.

COLIN. Don't give it another thought. Luggage doesn't really care about seeing Greece or Spain or Portugal. It'd prefer to sit in an air-conditioned department store. It's a tough life for luggage. I know, I'm an experienced luggage psychologist.

MONICA. Colin.

COLIN. I've talked them through abuse, intense job-related stress and even the trauma of being lost.

MONICA. You don't need to –

COLIN. I tell them about my fate theory. See, luggage doesn't really get lost. The person was just meant to go to the "other" place and didn't.

MONICA. That explains it. My luggage went to the right place, but I don't know where that is. And I feel fat.

COLIN. You're –

MONICA. Don't tell me I'm not. Agree with me.

COLIN. You look like you're feeling fat, even though you're not.

MONICA. The diplomatic meter just went way into the red zone.

AMANDA. *(as she enters)* I'm exhausted. I should have no problem sleeping on the plane.

MONICA. And I can't sleep. Maybe I should try a plane ride.

AMANDA. Colin, what did you do to her? She was unusually grumpy at the party today.

MONICA. All he did was be too nice. I did it to me. I planned your party the same day that I'm supposed to get my amnio results.

AMANDA. But I thought that was to keep your mind off –

MONICA. Well, it backfired and my mind is making up all kinds of horrible possibilities.

COLIN. It's just a couple more hours. Want me to call and see if – ?

MONICA. No. Please. I feel walls closing in on me…My whole life could change today and I want –

AMANDA. Your whole life has changed already. It will again in four months.

HANK. They're going to tell you if it's a boy or girl?

MONICA. Yes.

HANK. That'll ruin everything.

AMANDA. You don't have to look. They put a separate envelope with the sex written in it.

HANK. That was the most wonderful part of seeing you two born. Half the miracle is discovering that the new life is a boy or girl. You shouldn't have a crystal ball that lets you see inside there. God never intended for us to know ahead of time.

MONICA. *(looking at* **AMANDA***)* I know.

AMANDA. Don't look at me. God guided the doctors and gave them the skill to devise these tests.

MONICA. Pop, it would kill me to know that someone else knew and that I didn't. To know that envelope is sitting in a file somewhere with an 'm' or 'f' in it, would eat me alive.

HANK. Suit yourself. I know it's a girl anyway. You look just like your mother did when she was carrying you. Same shape, same feel, same sickness.

(beat)

AMANDA. You mean, *morning* sickness.

HANK. Yeah.

MONICA. Well, the amnio isn't the reason I'm a nervous wreck and why my life may change today.

AMANDA. What is?

MONICA. They may be able to tell me if the gene is present in the baby.

COLIN. What?

AMANDA. How?

MONICA. I'm not sure, but evidently they can isolate that certain chromosome and if it matches Daddy's and not Mother's, home free.

AMANDA. Amazing.

COLIN. I'll say. You knew about this possible detection and didn't tell any...one?

MONICA. I know. It's incredibly selfish of me. But I had a fleeting moment of sheer bravery and I've been in denial since. Don't hate me.

COLIN. That explains why you were so cantankerous at your party. So, why are you even bothering to tell us now?

MONICA. Because I'm scared.

(JEANNETTE *dances in. She looks dazed, lost.* **MONICA** *crosses to her and wipes saliva off her chin. Then* **JEANNETTE** *dances away.*)

HANK. You can handle whatever comes. You always have.

MONICA. Mother seems distant.

HANK. Yeah.

MONICA. I thought she'd be so happy about being a grandma.

HANK. She is, I suppose. But I think she's bitter because she won't really be able to help.

MONICA. Not in the traditional way, but –

HANK. I'll go check on her. (*He exits.*)

MONICA. (*to* **AMANDA**) Hey, what time does your car get here?

AMANDA. Two hours. God, Nick. If I'd known that you were going to find out –

MONICA. It's okay. I just planned this a little too close. Now, weren't you going to take a long, hot soaky bath before your limo arrives?

AMANDA. Yeah, but...Oh, God. I don't even feel like going now, Nick.

MONICA. Oh, don't pull that. No way. Your tub awaits.

AMANDA. Well, thank you two for such a great send off. It's –

MONICA. Standard procedure now for all our life-long employees before they take their first vacation in twenty years.

(**AMANDA** *starts to pick up confetti.*)

Go plunge. Your adventure begins...now!

AMANDA. I hate to leave. *(MONICA glares at her.)* Okay *(She exits.)*

COLIN. I just realized she's going to miss the benefit.

MONICA. All the work's done. Someone has to be there to put out little ego fires, that's all. *(She yawns.)*

COLIN. Why don't you try to take a nap? I'll wake you before –

MONICA. Now, you see? There's a perfect opportunity. Instead of kindly asking me if I want to take a nap, why don't you just come out and say: "Monica, you look like a pig-faced zombie. Go throw your blubber in bed."

COLIN. If you want to get mad at me, I'll just hit you.

MONICA. Please. I feel like I'm this bloated time bomb you have to handle so gingerly.

COLIN. You self-centered mega-bitch. I'm sick of hearing you gripe in between stuffing your fat face with gross amounts of disgusting slop. If you didn't have a hoglet inside you, I'd kick – *(He stops, a grin breaking across his face.)*

MONICA. That's a step in the right direction. Now you have to say it like you mean it.

COLIN. I can't. I just can't say…The only mean thing I can do is leave.

MONICA. And not call.

COLIN. Do you want me to?

MONICA. No. See? If you do it because I want you to, you're doing it to be nice.

COLIN. I see. *(He just stands there, lost.)*

MONICA. The problem is, I don't deserve you. And all I can think of every time you do something nice or say something considerate – which happens non-stop – is that you're wasted on me.

COLIN. True.

MONICA. That's better. *(They look at each other and finally **MONICA** smiles. She moves away.)* No. I don't want to take a nap. I want…

(**JEANNETTE** *waltzes in and dances over to the luggage. She carries a pressed rose and tries to insert it into the luggage and knocks it over.*)

MONICA. Mother! Be careful! Here. I'll slip it in for you. (*She opens a bag and slips the rose in.*) There.

COLIN. It was a great party, Mrs G. You would have been proud.

(**JEANNETTE** *goes to Mandy's desk and hits it, shaking her head.*)

MONICA. Mom, we've hired two temps to replace Mandy. She's already trained them. Don't worry. We'll be fine.

(**JEANNETTE** *waltzes out, shaking her head. A Knock is heard and* **ERROL** *enters wearing glasses and a suit.*)

ERROL. Hey, am I late?

MONICA. Depends on for what. If you came for the party, you're four hours late. If you came for the bubble bath, you're right on time.

ERROL. (*to* **MONICA**) You look great.

MONICA. You look different.

ERROL. No. I mean it. You been out in the sun?

COLIN. No, Errol. The pregnancy makes her heart beat faster and it gives her a rosy glow.

ERROL. I knew that. I was just trying to schmooze –

(**AMANDA** *enters wearing a bathrobe.*)

AMANDA. I thought I heard a strange (*sees* **ERROL**) but familiar voice. What brings you here?

ERROL. I was invited.

AMANDA. (*to* **MONICA**) To my bon voyage party?

MONICA. Yes.

AMANDA. (*to* **MONICA**) Did you give him the wrong time on purpose? (*to* **COLIN**) She's pulled that before.

ERROL. No. I just couldn't…get here sooner.

AMANDA. They have you working on Saturdays, huh? I guess you must have gotten that assistantship. You sure hose down good.

ERROL. Actually, no.

AMANDA. She didn't succumb to the tight khaki? Is she blind?

ERROL. She hired a girl.

AMANDA. Makes sense. Why be tempted eight hours a day? Who could get any work done? *(beat)* Well, surely you got promoted. It's been what, two months?

ERROL. Yeah. Something like that.

(**MONICA** *smiles at* **ERROL** *and crosses to the luggage and softly caresses it.*)

AMANDA. The glasses are a good choice. People will take you more seriously.

ERROL. Oh. I'm just wearing these because I got an eye infection and my contacts got grounded.

AMANDA. Poor babies.

ERROL. And I'm not at William Morris anymore.

MONICA. Ooh. Did the competition lure you away? Hope you got them into a bloody bidding war.

ERROL. Actually to tell the truth, I'm driving limo's now.

COLIN. No.

AMANDA. But –

MONICA. What?

ERROL. In fact, I'm taking you to the airport today.

AMANDA. This is too weird. What happened to Errol-the-super-agent?

ERROL. Well, all my buddies in the mailroom convinced me that I was on the wrong end of the picture and resume sending scene. I should be delivered and not delivering. So they sent some out and I got an acting job.

COLIN. But do you have any experience acting?

ERROL. No, but I think that helped.

MONICA. Was it softcore or hard?

AMANDA. Monica!

ERROL. Neither. It's a TV movie.

MONICA. Good God. A star is hatched. Let us know when you're ready for a press representative. We'll give you a discount.

AMANDA. And so you're driving cars in between – ?

ERROL. Yeah. Funny, huh?

MONICA. Mandy. You'd better hit the tub if you're going to –

AMANDA. Right. *(to* **ERROL***)* Thanks for coming by. I…

ERROL. See, I saw your name on the schedule and worked it so I could do you and have my lunch right before. But I had to miss the party.

AMANDA. Well, there's still some sushi left. I've got to get in the tub before I get dressed.

*(***ERROL*** starts to get undressed.)*

COLIN. What kind of limo service is this?

AMANDA. Listen, Err, babe. This isn't –

ERROL. I'll just scrub your back. But I can't get the uniform wet.

AMANDA. It's a Jean Nate bubble bath. You'll smell like –

ERROL. Who cares? I'll borrow some of Hank's "Right Guard." *(He winks at* **COLIN** *and* **MONICA** *as they exit.)*

MONICA. I love it when people surprise me. I've never surprised anyone.

COLIN. You surprised me when you told me you were expecting.

MONICA. Did I really?

COLIN. Yeah.

MONICA. But I told you, the first time we met, that I wanted to bear your children.

COLIN. But that's an old line. Nobody means it.

MONICA. I did. I didn't know that I'd fall into – whatever it is we've fallen into.

COLIN. You can't say "love?"

MONICA. There's just so many other things whisking around in me with my high hormone level, it's hard to tell.

COLIN. All right. Take it from your impartial, obsessed, sexual slave, we have love.

MONICA. You know, of course, that I am the way I am because I was purposely careless.

COLIN. Knowing the way you are with kids, I suspected as much.

MONICA. Does that bother you?

COLIN. Should it?

MONICA. Well, it's a little calculated, cold-hearted, controlling –

COLIN. A little?

MONICA. A lot.

COLIN. What's the matter, Monica? You seem scattered –

MONICA. Oh, please. Don't let that evil, sensitive fiancé out! Keep him –

COLIN. A blind truck driver couldn't help notice – Come on. What's –

MONICA. I don't know. I see Mother look longingly at the luggage and I remember she and Daddy were going to fly around the world ten times; just as soon as we could run the agency. She had clothes and hats put away for their trip. She still does. I see Mandy getting ready to take on a new adventure. Errol Flynn's changed careers like someone else changes golf clubs and I'm in quicksand. I'm getting heavier by the minute. And you're standing there, holding out a hand to save me the second I look helpless and I want to go through that quicksand and start over.

COLIN. All right. Here's something you don't want to hear. Here's something insensitive. Aren't you feeling a little too sorry for yourself?

MONICA. No, Godammit. I'm frustrated and I want to do something about it. I want out. I want a change.

COLIN. You're right in the middle of a very big change.

MONICA. No, before that. I have such a short time ahead of me and I want to make it all count. I'll love having this baby, but I don't want to resent him for robbing me of…

COLIN. Of what?

MONICA. An adventure...Yes! *My* adventure! *(yelling)* Amanda!

COLIN. What are you talking about?

MONICA. *(yelling)* Mandy!

AMANDA. *(offstage)* What?

MONICA. Come here! *(Looking at **COLIN**)* No, I couldn't. Yes, I could. I actually could.

*(**HANK** enters sleepily.)*

HANK. Can't a person start a nap without some disaster befalling – What is it?

*(**ERROL** and **AMANDA** enter dressed in towels.)*

AMANDA. What? What?

HANK. *(Noting **AMANDA** and **ERROL**)* Holy Toledo! How long have I been asleep?

ERROL. Hi, Mr. G.

MONICA. *(to **AMANDA**)* I forgot you were taking a bath.

AMANDA. Obviously. What is it? Is there something wrong about the benefit? You know you're going to have to get used to –

MONICA. No. Can I borrow your ticket?

AMANDA. My ticket? Ticket to what?

MONICA. To Europe.

AMANDA. Mandy. You're not making any sense. I gave you the itinerary.

MONICA. No shithead. I want to go in your place.

AMANDA. Let me get the bubbles out of my ear. Did you say – ?

MONICA. I'll be "A. Glendenning" instead of 'M.'

AMANDA. But I – I've been...

MONICA. I'll only ask once. I know it's a huge, monstrous request and it's totally selfish. But it is spontaneous. Once Dylan comes, I'll never be able to...Whereas you could.

AMANDA. But I'm all packed and...

MONICA. Stay packed.

AMANDA. You're not.

MONICA. I'll get something over there. Nothing I have fits anyway.

COLIN. This is a joke, right? All of it, the lonely luggage bit, Errol-the-quick-change-chauffeur –

MONICA. No! It's real. I'm going to go blind sightseeing.

AMANDA. But you're pregnant.

MONICA. So? It's only dangerous in the ninth month. I'll be back by then.

AMANDA. Monica, think this through. At least wait until you get the results from –

MONICA. No, I can't. *(She looks at* **COLIN***, who smiles.)* That's exactly what I should do, but…

AMANDA. What about the benefit? All that work you've put into it.

MONICA. I'm done. You can put out the fires. Mandy, please. Be the wonderfully flexible person I know you are.

AMANDA. No! You can't run away from the answer.

MONICA. That's not what I'm trying to do! Godammit. I just want an adventure before…I settle…You guys, I – *(She stops.)*

ERROL. Yeah! I think this'd be a good time to get bathrobes. *(He exits.)*

COLIN. *(to* **MONICA***)* Should we get Dr. Mendoza on the phone?

MONICA. She won't tell us anything. We have to go in.

AMANDA. We could try.

*(***MONICA** *nods.* **AMANDA** *speed dials the number and hands the phone to* **MONICA***, who can't touch it.)*

AMANDA. *(into phone)* Yes, I've got Colin McMann for Dr. Mendoza…He's the father of Monica Glendenning's baby…Yes…

HANK. Nettie! *(He exits to retrieve* **JEANNETTE***.)*

*(***ERROL** *re-enters dressed in a bathrobe and wrapes one around* **AMANDA***.)*

AMANDA. *(Into phone)* Dr. Mendoza, can you hold for Mr. McMann?...Thank you. *(to* **COLIN***)* She's all yours. *(She hands the phone to* **COLIN***.)*

COLIN. *(into phone)* Dr. Mendoza?...Thank you...Yes, well, I'm here with her now and I don't think she's up to coming to your office...I can appreciate that...Of course...Can you make an exception?...Doctor, you'll have to admit these are extenuating circumstances and –

*(***MONICA** *picks up a different phone and punches into the call.)*

MONICA. *(into phone)* Doctor, it's Monica.

*(***HANK & JEANNETTE** *enter).*

This is not a schedule thing like I've pulled every time before. Everyone I'd want to celebrate or commiserate with is here now. So...I'll come in later, of course...

*(***AMANDA** *and* **HANK** *pick up extensions.)*

MONICA. *(into phone)* Yes, start with the amnio...Oh, God. *(She holds* **COLIN***'s hand.)* Everything's okay? Really?... Thank God...Uh huh...Yes, we want to know, don't we Colin?

COLIN. *(into phone)* Yes.

MONICA & COLIN. A boy! Yes!

ERROL. Way to go, Colin! Well, he had something to do with it being a boy, right?

MONICA. *(to* **COLIN***)* Dylan! *(to* **HANK***)* Fooled you, Daddy!

MONICA. *(into phone)* Okay. Now, the chromosome test. *(beat)* The baby's clear? He won't get Huntington's? Oh, my God.

(She drops the phone and looks as if she might faint. **AMANDA** *hangs up and crosses to* **MONICA***).*

(to **AMANDA***)* Clear. What a beautiful word.

(They embrace.)

COLIN. *(into phone)* Yes, thank you, Doctor...Yeah...We will, I promise. Thanks for, well, bending the rules this time...Bye. *(He hangs up.)*

HANK. Nicky, that's terrific! *(He embraces* **MONICA.**)

*(***ERROL** *and* **COLIN** *stand in line to embrace* **MONICA.** **JEANNETTE** *dances joyfully, removed from the others.)*

MONICA. What is this, kiss the bride time?

AMANDA. You tell us.

MONICA. Errol, you bring good luck.

(She embraces **ERROL**, *then pushes him away and looks at* **COLIN**, *who slowly embraces her).*

Thank you for making the call, I know how you hate the phone. Mother? *(She crosses to* **JEANNETTE**.*)* We're going to have a healthy grandkid.

(She tries to embrace **JEANNETTE**, *but* **JEANNETTE** *is too excited and they cannot connect.)*

(They all stand there not knowing what to say.)

MONICA. What's the matter? How come you're all looking at me so strangely?

AMANDA. I've never seen you this calm.

MONICA. Really? Yeah. You know what? You know what? I actually feel – I do, I feel lighter. Isn't that weird? I feel like this huge weight has been lifted. God. I haven't felt better about anything in…It's, it's like a sliding closet door that's off the track. You keep tugging and pulling and it won't glide. I just got on track. It's a short track, but a smooth ride.

*(***MONICA** *stops and looks at everyone watching her.)*

MONICA. I'm not making sense, am I? But it just all opened up in front of me. A clear path. And do you know what I want? I want to take that trip. Is that horribly selfish of me?

AMANDA. Yes. But it's also very 'Monica' of you.

MONICA. And I want to take it for her and…for me.

*(***JEANNETTE** *exits, puzzled.)*

COLIN. You think you'd want to be in Europe all alone?

MONICA. Go? Yes. I want to go to the airport all by myself, get on the plane alone and arrive…arrive all by myself.

AMANDA. You know what though? I just don't feel right having you leave today. Let me call and see what the penalties are to postpone a week.

MONICA. Not a week!

AMANDA. A few days.

MONICA. One or two.

ERROL. God, I've missed you guys. No one in my family's like this!

AMANDA. Be thankful. *(beat, then to* **MONICA***)* You know, you might feel really calm if you went ahead and found out about you.

ERROL. *(to* **MONICA***)* You want me to call? Maybe my good luck will rub off on the phone and they'll accidentally tell me.

MONICA. *(laughing)* You know what? They keep that information locked up tighter and the plans for the newest stealth bomber. And Errol could probably just call up and find out.

ERROL. What's the number?

MONICA. No. I'm a very conservative gambler. We won…a little. And I can't go back to the table. I'd rather walk away a winner.

HANK. You are a winner, Nicky. *(He embraces her.)*

ERROL. Oh, shit. What am I going to do about the limo?

AMANDA. Relax. You'll be included in the cancellation fees. Come on. *(She and* **ERROL** *exit.)*

HANK. Nick, Nettie feels left out or something.

MONICA. Tell her to come down. I'll talk to her.

*(***HANK*** exits.)*

COLIN. How long do you plan to be gone?

MONICA. I don't know. Don't hold me to anything.

COLIN. But you'll be back before your ninth?

*(***MONICA*** nods.)*

COLIN. I thought we were going to get married before Dylan was born and go to Lamaze classes and –

MONICA. Maybe we will, maybe we…You see? I can't plan. For once in my life, I will not plan.

COLIN. Nicky, wouldn't you want to share some of this adventure?

MONICA. *(She takes off the engagement ring.)* Bring this to me. Propose to me somewhere exotic – surprise me. Oh, shit. You see? There I go planning a surprise. You do whatever you want.

COLIN. Okay.

MONICA. I don't even have a suitcase.

COLIN. You want to borrow one of my duffels? You could trash it if you buy –

MONICA. Yes. You have one in the car?

COLIN. Always. *(MONICA looks at him.)* Do I know you?

MONICA. Want to?

COLIN. Yeah. Oh, yeah. *(kisses her)*

(JEANNETTE enters carrying a hat and waltzes in place. COLIN and MONICA break and he runs off. JEANNETTE gives the hat to MONICA.)

MONICA. Thank you, Mother. I'll wear this in Paris. *(She sets it on the luggage. Beat.)* I'm taking this trip for us. So that when I'm where you are, I'll at least know that I travelled the world once.

(JEANNETTE waltzes up to MONICA and pats the baby. MONICA removes her hand.)

I'll take good care of Dylan. He's just going to sample a lot of great food…unimported.

(JEANNETTE waltzes upstage and turns away from MONICA and dances in place.)

Mom, for the first time in a very long time, I feel alive because I don't know what's coming next.

(JEANNETTE turns and opens her arms to MONICA.)

But Mother, I…I need you.

(MONICA *moves to* JEANNETTE *and holds her tightly.* JEANNETTE *remains still. Then slowly,* MONICA *begins to sway.* JEANNETTE *sways with her, easily, comfortably.* MONICA *smiles.*)

(*Lights fade and silhouette* JEANNETTE *and* MONICA. *Slowly, gracefully lights fade out.*)

(*Curtain.*)

PROPERTIES

ACT I, Scene 1

(Monica)
Mailing List Print-out
Rolodex

(Amanda)
Kiwi plant with Kangaroo (stuffed animal)

(Hank)
Glass of water
Box of envelopes
Office supplies (pens, notepads, post-it notes, etc.)
Videos
Fresh flowers (white roses)
Large covered drinking glass with thick straw

(Colin)
Shopping bag with library books and assorted folders with Xeroxed news articles

ACT I, Scene 2

(Colin)
2 scrapbooks

(Monica)
2 dessert plates and forks
2 wine glasses

(Amanda)
Test results (in medical-looking envelope)

ACT II, Scene 1

(Hank)
stacks of envelopes
papers to fold
sponge tray for sealing envelopes

(Jeannette)
Assorted pieces of incoming mail
Small cassette recorder and earphones

(Amanda)
Coffee Mug
Pink Lipstick

ACT II, Scene 2

(Amanda)
Plastic sheets with slides
Box of printed invitations from printer

(Monica)
Book of baby names

(Colin)
Carrot sticks
Duffel bag containing Chinese Food container with rigged fortune cookie that has engagement ring in it. [Actor may need to do "sleight of hand" trick if cookie cannot be rigged]

(Jeannette)
Baby stroller filled with framed pictures and baby doll and torn-up photographs
Baby rattle

ACT II, Scene 3

(Amanda)
Packed suitcases)

(Jeannette)
Pressed rose
Hat

COSTUMES

ACT I, Scene 1

MONICA – business attire, casual
AMANDA – casual
JEANNETTE – nightgown, silk robe, slippers
HANK – casual tracksuit
COLIN – cargo pants, workshirt and multi-pocketed vest
ERROL – blue dress shirt & tie, black jeans

ACT I, Scene 2

MONICA – nice evening clothes
AMANDA – fun evening clothes
JEANNETTE – nightgown, silk robe, slippers
HANK – boxer shorts & Hawaiian shirt
COLIN – slacks, knit-shirt, jacket (on chair)
ERROL – casual evening clothes

ACT II, Scene 1

MONICA – business attire, casual
AMANDA – kimono, slippers
JEANNETTE – nightgown, silk robe, slippers
HANK – casual tracksuit

ACT II, Scene 2

MONICA – business attire, casual
AMANDA – cute short dress
JEANNETTE – nightgown, silk robe, slippers
HANK – jogging clothes, terrycloth robe
COLIN – black jeans, shirt, shoes
ERROL – work-out shorts, tank top

ACT II, Scene 3

MONICA – business attire, dressy
AMANDA – party dress; later bathrobe
JEANNETTE – nightgown, silk robe, slippers
HANK – jeans and subtle Hawaiian shirt
COLIN – slacks and knit-shirt
ERROL – 3-piece business suit, glasses; later a towel

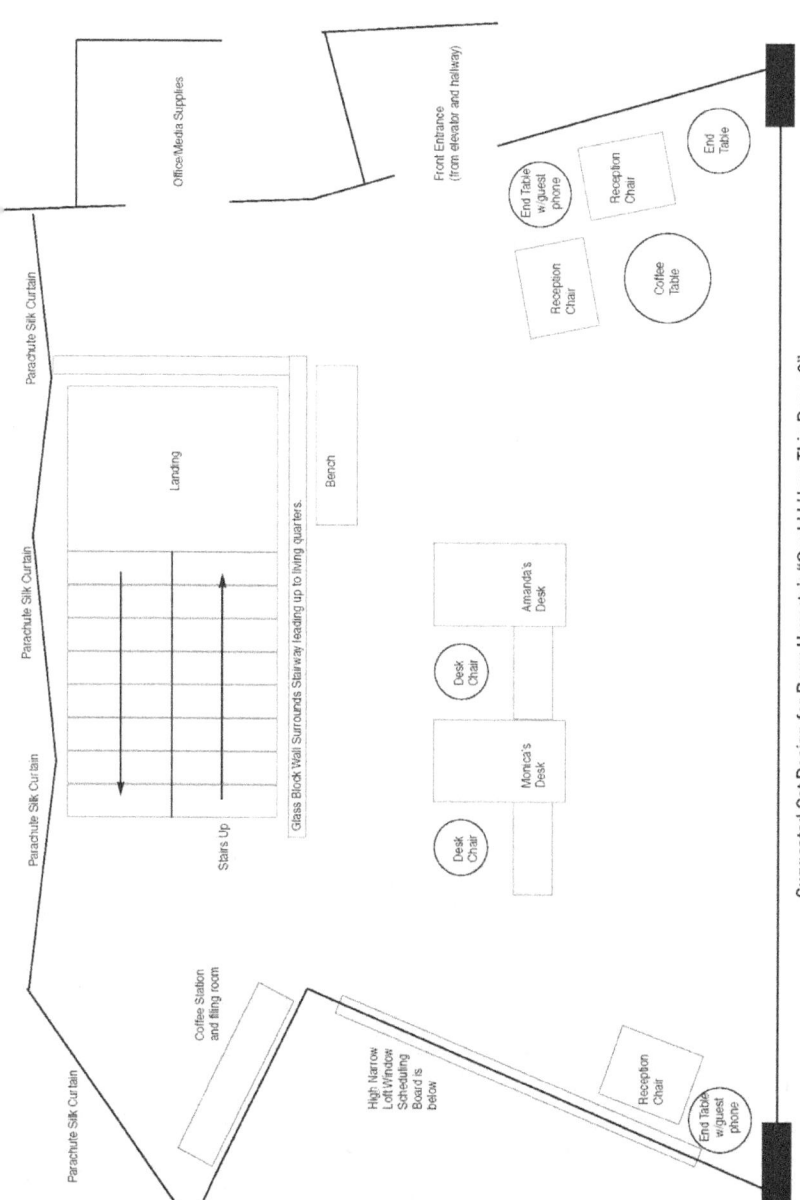

Suggested Set Design for Doug Haverty's "Could I Have This Dance?"

From the Reviews of
COULD I HAVE THIS DANCE?...

"Playwright Doug Haverty uses Huntington's Disease not in the telepic fashion where the disability is the star, but as a vehicle to explore human nature...The play is kind of cross between Lee Blessing's *Independence* and Arthur Kopit's *Wings*...Every character has color and dimension."
- *Variety*

"In a profound blend of pathos and humor, the memorable world premiere of Doug Haverty's drama repeatedly transports the audience from out right hilarity to heartfelt sorrow...Electrifying...This show is one of the season's best."
- *Los Angeles Reader*

"A gripping, emotional piece that both educates and enlightens...Haverty's story is engaging and informative, his dialogue crisp and humorous. The characters are interesting and well-developed...The strength of family-in-crisis is always what gives one renewed hope. *Could I Have This Dance?*, takes that strength and provides a courageous arena for its expression."
- *The Burbank Times*

"Outstanding in every way...a very sensitive portrayal of Huntington's Disease...Haverty has written a delicate story, yet places humor along the way so this dramatization does not come off as a death mask or heavy drama filled with sadness...(A) well written play...This is one you should not miss."
- *The Tolucan*

"Haverty has tackled a very serious subject and delivered it in a play that also entertains...(He) has written a sophisticated story about relationships without preaching about the disease. He doesn't have to. It's underneath everything...a very interesting new play!"
- *The Daily Breeze*

"Haverty knows of what he writes and has transferred both his knowledge and heart to a text that pulls no punches."
- *L.A. Weekly*

"*Could I Have This Dance?*, under Doug Haverty's deft, comic hand is a story about the uncertainty of life. It's about the war of fate and genetics."
- *Los Angeles Daily News*

"Doug Haverty has written a beautifully touching, achingly funny and informative play about the effects of Huntington's Disease on family members...Haverty's craftsman-like writing and Jules Aaron's skillful direction never let the facts and figures overwhelm the delicate story or let the pathos become bathos...wonderful experience."
- *Frontiers*

"Doug Haverty's excellent play deals with a good deal more than illness...*Could I Have This Dance?*, sparkles like fine champagne, but never intoxicates—though most people who see it will feel happy for hours after they leave the theatre—for in addition to its humanity, it is a damn funny play...The ultimate power of *Could I Have This Dance?*, though, for all the exceptional work of this gifted company, rests in Doug Haverty's considerable skill as a playwright...Extraordinary from first moment to last."
- *Drama-Logue*

"An important new play...very intelligently written and also a solidly entertaining play... Witty lines and funny situations provide plenty of comic relief before the action becomes heavy...Haverty's grasp of contemporary dialogue is right on the money. His ability to write female chatter and emotions comes as no surprise to those familiar with his previous outings...Both comical and poignant in context."
- *News-Press*

"What we're treated to—an increasingly rare treat—is how they handle this reality and their own emotions...Haverty has an uncluttered sense of character and a good ear for snappy dialogue...Haverty's people are down-to-earth and in touch with their feelings. They also speak their minds with sobering candor...The welcome pattern of sanity than runs through this bantering piece leaves you in the end with a bit of a glow and wishing there were more of this up front kind of coping in real life. There is nothing so attractive or refreshing as people who can face whatever life dishes up and deal with it. That singular element makes Haverty's unexpectedly urbane play a surprise as well as a joy."
- *The Los Angeles Times*

**Also by
Doug Haverty...**

In My Mind's Eye
Inside Out (A Musical)

Please visit our website **samuelfrench.com** for complete descriptions and licensing information

www.ingramcontent.com/pod-product-compliance
Lightning Source LLC
Chambersburg PA
CBHW070647300426
44111CB00013B/2300